The Greater and Lesser Mysteries of Christianity

The Complementary Paths of Anthroposophy and Catholicism

RON MACFARLANE

Published 2015 by
Greater Mysteries Publications
Mission, BC, Canada

Cover Design: Ron MacFarlane

Printed in the United States of America

ISBN:
ISBN-13: 978-0994007766
ISBN-10: 0994007760

DEDICATION

This work is reverently dedicated to the Bodhisattva-Zarathustra (known esoterically as the "Master Jesus"), for his dedicated and faithful guardianship of the Christian Church throughout the difficult and turbulent centuries.

CONTENTS

THE GREATER

AND LESSER MYSTERIES

OF CHRISTIANITY

INTRODUCTION

CONTEMPORARY CHRISTIANITY, the world religion established by the God-Man, Christ-Jesus, and founded on the revelatory-principle that "God is love," is hardly the shining example of ideological unity and universal brotherhood that it was intended to be. There are approximately 41,000 different Christian denominations in the world today, many of which are fervently hostile to each other. Atheistic and anti-Christian polemicists have concluded that there is something inherently wrong with Christianity itself and, in consequence, it is doomed to failure and eventual extinction.

Discerning Christian advocates, however, know that any apparent failure to realize the high ideals of Christianity is not due to the profound teachings and the illustrious life-example of Christ-Jesus, but instead to the limitations of wounded human nature. Corrupt, power-hungry, destructive and evil-minded human beings have twisted, distorted and fragmented true Christianity for the past two thousand years, and continue to do so today.

Moreover, on a much deeper spiritual level, since Christianity is indeed a divinely-initiated endeavor to help restore "fallen" humanity, powerful and demonic beings have attempted to destroy nascent Christianity from its very inception. But thankfully, according to Christ-Jesus himself, "the powers of hell will not prevail against it [Christianity]" (Matt 16:18).

Sadly contributing to the injurious fragmentation of Christianity—the "religion of divine love"—is the sectarian hostility between certain proponents of anthroposophy and select members of the Catholic Church. In both cases, this is largely due to ignorance; that is, an almost complete lack of understanding about the true significance and mission of the other: anthroposophical critics know almost nothing of Catholicism; and Catholic critics know almost nothing about anthroposophy.

The wonderful reconciliatory fact is that anthroposophy and Catholicism are not conflicting polar opposites, but are instead like two sides of the same golden coin—different, but complementary. Instead of only one side or the other being the only true approach to Christ-Jesus, both are uniquely necessary and both positively contribute to the complete truth of Christianity.

Since this author is happily and harmoniously both an anthroposophist and a Catholic, *The Greater and Lesser Mysteries of Christianity: The Complementary Paths of Anthroposophy and Catholicism* earnestly seeks to correct the misinformation and lack of understanding that each partisan critic has for the other. As in almost every significant dispute, increased knowledge and familiarity about each other will in time bring both sides closer together for mutual growth and benefit.

CHAPTER 1

THE TWOFOLD DIVISION OF
CHRISTIAN KNOWLEDGE

1.1 Esoteric and Exoteric Christianity: The Greater and Lesser Mysteries of Christ-Jesus

UNFORTUNATELY, VEHEMENT anthroposophical critics of Catholicism and fervent Catholic critics of anthroposophy do not realize (and hence are entirely unaware) that Christ-Jesus separated the wisdom-teachings of Christianity into two distinct but complementary approaches. While on earth, he conveyed simplified mystery-truths in the form of parables and imaginative stories to the less-educated general population; but to his specially-trained disciples, he was able to convey more complex mystery-truths in clear, conceptual form. As biblically recorded in Matthew (13:10–13):

> Then the disciples came and said to him, "Why do you speak to them in parables?" And he answered them, "To you it has been given to know the secrets of the kingdom of heaven, but to them it has not been given. For to him

who has will more be given, and he will have abundance; but from him who has not, even what he has will be taken away. This is why I speak to them in parables, because seeing they do not see, and hearing they do not hear, nor do they understand.

After his crucifixion and resurrection, Christ-Jesus continued this twofold presentation of his Christian teachings; but in a more institutional way. St. Peter was chosen to institute a universal *religion* and *theology* in order to preserve, promulgate and impart the more simplified mystery-teachings of Christianity to the general population. This broad, widespread institutional approach can be termed, "exoteric Christianity." As well, the wisdom-teachings that are "less-complex," and intended for the "less-prepared" general population, can be termed, the "lesser mysteries."

St. John (the evangelist, not the apostle) was chosen to institute a universal *philosophy* and *theosophy* to preserve, promulgate and impart the more complex mystery-teachings of Christianity to specially-trained disciples. This select, more-exclusive institutional approach can be termed, "esoteric Christianity." As well, the wisdom-teachings that are "greater in complexity," and which require "greater preparation" from specially-trained disciples can be termed, the "greater mysteries" (please refer to Figure 1 on the following page).

In this case, the terms "greater" and "lesser" do not in any way imply "superior" and "inferior." Both forms of institutional Christian truth are equally profound and equally illuminating. Moreover, since both forms of wisdom-teaching issue from the God-Man, Christ-Jesus, they equally reflect supernal reality, and are therefore equally infused with divine potency. As such, the "lesser mysteries of exoteric Christianity" and the "greater mysteries of esoteric Christianity" both convey the sanctifying grace of the Holy Spirit of God, which has the divine power to purify and redeem our bodies and our souls.

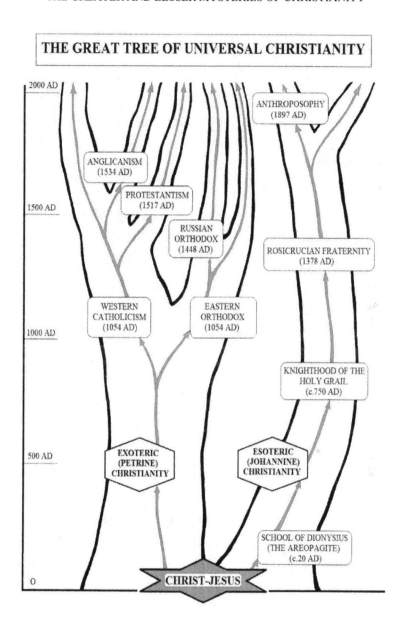

Figure 1: Esoteric and Exoteric Christianity

1.2 The Persecution of Esoteric Christianity by the Church of Rome

Even though these two institutional forms of Christianity were divinely intended to historically develop independently, they were also intended to amicably co-exist, and to beneficially support one another throughout time. Regrettably, when Emperor Theodosius I, in 380, declared Christianity (as defined by the First Council of Nicaea) to be the official state religion of the Roman Empire, he also declared that all other religious expressions were considered to be heretical and deserving of state persecution. In the words of the Edict of Thessalonica:

> We authorize the followers of this law to assume the title of Catholic Christians; but as for the others, since, in our judgment they are foolish madmen, we decree that they shall be branded with the ignominious name of heretics, and shall not presume to give to their conventicles the name of churches. They will suffer in the first place the chastisement of the divine condemnation and in the second the punishment of our authority which in accordance with the will of Heaven we shall decide to inflict.

From that point on, in the official eyes of the powerful Roman state, and in the equally-intolerant attitude of the Roman Catholic Church, any form of esoteric Christianity was considered to be heretical, and thereby open to lawful persecution. Consequently, for many centuries, institutional expressions of esoteric Christianity—such as the Knighthood of the Holy Grail and the Fraternity of the Rose-Cross—were forced to remain protectively hidden from public view and anonymously safe from hostile state scrutiny. To the detriment of true Christian development, without the broadening and uplifting inclusion of esoteric Christianity, outward historical development has been mainly one-sided and incomplete.

1.3 The Church Condemnation of Anthroposophy

Perhaps not surprisingly, then, when a modern-day form of esoteric Christianity, known as "anthroposophy," was publically established in 1912 by Austrian philosopher and esotericist, Rudolf Steiner (1861–1925), it was also very soon (in 1919) "condemned" by obdurate authorities within the Church of St. Peter.

This particular ecclesiastical condemnation, however, was more in the nature of "guilt by association," since the Church's censure was really directed at the teachings of the Theosophical Society. Since anthroposophy was originally associated with the Theosophical Society, the Church censurers considered Rudolf Steiner's teachings to be a "theosophical, neo-gnostic heresy" as well.

This, of course, is a clear demonstration by Church authorities of their complete lack of understanding regarding the content of anthroposophy, or of its history. Fact is, Rudolf Steiner broke away from the Theosophical Society and formed anthroposophy *because of* the heterodox, anti-Christian attitude and activities of Theosophy and its leaders. Moreover, Steiner made it very clear that anthroposophy was not a revival or renewal of pagan Gnosticism. In Steiner's own words:

> The Gnosis was strictly guarded in hidden Mysteries ... Anthroposophy cannot be a revival of the Gnosis. For the latter depended on the development of the Sentient Soul; while Anthroposophy must evolve out of the Spiritual Soul, in the light of Michael's activity, a new understanding of Christ and of the World. (Anthroposophical Leading Thoughts; "Gnosis and

Anthroposophy"; 1925)

1.4 Rudolf Steiner's Criticism of the Roman Catholic Church

Reciprocally, Rudolf Steiner in numerous lectures directed some very harsh criticism at the Roman Catholic Church as it existed in the late-nineteenth and early-twentieth century. Furthermore, his harshest diatribes were focused on rogue Jesuits within the Church who, he claimed, were intent on destroying anthroposophy. Steiner went so far as to reveal that certain Jesuits, in collusion with specific Freemasons, had intentionally burned down the large, double-domed anthroposophical building constructed in Dornach, Switzerland, known as the "Johannesbau" (the House of St. John) on New Year's Eve, 31 December 1922 (–1 January 1923). In an esoteric lesson given to the "Wachsmuth-Lerchenfeld group" in May 1923, Steiner stated:

> This harmonious union of two movements that are otherwise hostile to each other [the Jesuits and Freemasons] led to the destruction of the Johannes Building.

In another lecture given on 30 July 1918 entitled, "Problems of the Time," Steiner even implicated the Jesuits in the underlying causes of World War I:

> These two currents of thought, Americanism and Jesuitism, play into one another, as it were. This is not something to take casually; and all such matters we must look for the deeper impulses which are active in human evolution. If we try to identify the forces which have brought about the present catastrophe [World War I], we shall find [a] remarkable cooperation between Americanism—in a sense here given—and Jesuitism.

Regarding the Roman Catholic Church, itself, Steiner's position seems to be that it was relevant and contributory during the Graeco-Roman cultural era; but since that era ended in the middle of the fifteenth century (with the beginning of the Renaissance), the Church is now an historical anomaly, and therefore destined to disappear:

> [T]he Roman Catholic Church represents the last remnant of what was the right civilization for the fourth post-Atlantean epoch [the Graeco-Roman era], what was justified right up to the middle of the Fifteenth Century, but what has now become a shadow. Of course products of a later evolution often herald their arrival in an earlier period, and its earlier products linger on into a later epoch; but in essentials the Roman Catholic Church represents what was justifiable for Europe and its colonies up to the middle of the Fifteenth Century. (Lecture given on 3 June 1920 entitled, "Roman Catholicism")

1.5 Any Hope of Reconciling Anthroposophy and Catholicism?

It certainly appears from what has been outline thus far, that there is no love lost between anthroposophy and Catholicism—so, is there any possibility of reconciling the two positions, of bringing them into an amicable relationship?

Not only is it possible; but, more importantly—it is imperative—since continued mutual disdain and polarization is seriously detrimental to the crucial salvational mission of true Christianity.

Much of the anthroposophical criticism of Catholicism is easily dissipated by an increased understanding of current Catholic teaching, and by recognizing the fact that the Catholic Church of today is a whole lot different than it was in the late-nineteenth and early-twentieth centuries. Few anthroposophists know anything about Catholicism or the modern-day Church, and yet unquestioningly apply Rudolf Steiner's century-old criticisms to the ecclesiastical conditions of today. For instance, it will no doubt come as an utter surprise and shock to anthroposophical critics to learn that the contemporary Jesuits are diametrically and radically different than they were a hundred years ago when Steiner was alive.

Reciprocally, in dealing with the contemporary Catholic condemnation of anthroposophy, an increased understanding of the essential teachings of spiritual science will certainly allay any concerns or fears of the Church that anthroposophy is somehow a religious, heretical threat. It is also conciliatory to note and to recognize that in many recorded instances Rudolf Steiner expressed very high regard for the historical importance and continuous contributions of the Catholic Church.

Moreover, future amicable harmony between the Catholic Church and anthroposophy will naturally occur when more and more critics from both sides come to understand and accept the twofold division of Christian teaching into esoteric and exoteric Christianity. Once it is widely recognized that both approaches are mutually necessary; but that they also require a healthy, developmental autonomy, then a more peaceful and beneficial co-existence will certainly arise.

CHAPTER 2

RUDOLF STEINER'S LIFELONG CONNECTION TO CATHOLICISM

2.1 Rudolf Steiner's Catholic Baptism

MANY ANTHROPOSOPHISTS, and certain Catholic authorities, have concluded from Rudolf Steiner's many critical statements concerning the Church of St. Peter that he was decidedly anti-Catholic. As an unfortunate result, many contemporary, blindly-accepting anthroposophical followers subconsciously maintain an unjustified, anti-Catholic disposition. But as the facts clearly demonstrate, Rudolf Steiner's life and upbringing was deeply rooted in Catholicism.

On 27 February 1861, as a newborn infant, Rudolf Steiner was baptized Catholic in St. Michael's Church in Draskovec (in modern-day Croatia). Though he was born a little over a day before in neighbouring Kraljevec, due to a mishandled delivery, there was some uncertainty as to whether the infant would survive; hence the emergency baptism so soon after birth.

Being baptized a Catholic meant that for his entire life, in the eyes of the Catholic Church, Rudolf Steiner remained a Catholic. The Church, then and now, regards baptism as one of the seven sacred sacraments established by Christ-Jesus on earth. When properly administered, baptism is fundamentally believed to possess the efficacious power (through the intercession of the Holy Spirit) to remove the stain of original sin on human nature. Since this particular sacrament, then, leaves an indelible mark upon the receptive Christian soul, baptism can be properly received only once in life.

If, as an adult, one decides not to practice the Faith or to not attend weekly Mass, that does not mean that one is no longer a Catholic. In those cases, one is considered to be a "non-practicing Catholic"; but a Catholic, nonetheless. Even in the case of becoming a member of another denomination, say Presbyterian, one is regarded as a "fallen-away Catholic"; but still a Catholic. Even after receiving the serious censure of "excommunication," though the recipient is 'out of communion' with the Church (and therefore disallowed from receiving 'Holy Communion' during Mass), they still remain a Catholic. At any time, the excommunicating offense can be forgiven (through the sacrament of penance and reconciliation; that is, through Holy Confession), and the offending individual restored to full participation in the Church.

From the foregoing examples, it is clear that the oft-heard expression: "Once a Catholic, always a Catholic," is not just an empty phrase—the fact of which applies to Rudolf Steiner as well.

2.2   Young Rudolf Steiner as Devoted Altar Server

When Rudolf Steiner was eight years old, his family moved to Neudörfl, a small village then in Hungary (but now in

Austria). While attending school there, the young Rudolf became familiar with the village priest, Fr. Franz Maraz, who taught religious classes at the school twice a week. Rudolf grew quite fond of the priest and decided to become an altar server in the local church. This was very much a heartfelt, independent decision on Rudolf's part, since his father, Johann, was at that time a staunch, non-practicing Catholic and vocal critic of the Austrian priesthood (though he later returned to a "pious life" in his old age).

As an altar server, young Rudolf willingly assisted at Masses, funerals and Corpus Christi processions.[1] Even though he wasn't particularly interested in Bible study or in catechism (Catholic instruction) classes, the sensitive, clairvoyant soul[2] of young Rudolf was deeply stirred by the liturgical rituals of the Mass. As he later shared in his autobiography, *The Course of My Life* (1986):

> The solemnity of the Latin language and of the liturgy was a thing in which my boyish soul found a vital happiness ...
>
> Out of my boyhood at Neudorfl I have the strongest impression of the way in which the contemplation of the rites of the church, in connection with the solemnity of liturgical music, causes the riddles of existence to rise in powerful suggestive fashion before the mind. The instruction in the Bible and the catechism imparted by the priest had far less effect upon my inner world than what he accomplished as celebrant of the cultus in mediating between the sensible and the supersensible world. From the first, all this was to me no mere form, but a profound experience.

From the preceding quotation, it is clear that, even as a young boy, Rudolf Steiner was able to experience and acknowledge the supersensible elements of the Catholic Mass, especially the miraculous events of the Eucharist (Holy

Communion).

2.3 The Profound Influences of Catholic Priests and Monks During Steiner's Formative Years

As a young boy, Rudolf Steiner was very fond of the village priest of Neudörfl, Fr. Franz Maraz, not only for his religious participation in the Mass, but also for his scientific instruction in astronomy and Copernican heliocentric theory. Both of these areas would have an enduring, lifelong influence in Steiner's life.

> Next to the assistant teacher, the person whom I loved most among those who had to do with the direction of the school was the priest ... Among the persons whom I came to know up to my tenth or eleventh year, he was by far the most significant ...
>
> I owe to this priest also, because of a certain profound impression made upon me, a great deal in the later orientation of my intellectual life. (Ibid.)

In Rudolf Steiner's day, there were two different secondary school systems available in Austria and Germany: the "realschule" (which emphasized science and literature) and the "gymnasium" (which emphasized the humanities). Highly-educated and well-respected priest-monks of the Cistercian Order[3] were very much involved in secondary education at that time (particularly in the gymnasiums). As a result, young Rudolf Steiner was very much influenced by Cistercian educators who were everywhere present in his immediate surroundings. As he stated in his autobiography:

> I grew up, so to speak, in the shadow of the Cistercian Order, which has important settlements in the neighbourhood of Wiener-Neustadt. Those who had to educate most of the youth in the district where I grew up,

were priests of the Cistercian Order. I had the robe of this order perpetually before me, the white robe with the black band around the waist, or, as we call it, the stola. Had I had the occasion to speak of such things in my autobiography I could have said: everything in my life tended in a classical education [in the humanities] at the Gymnasium and not of that modern education which I underwent in the Realschule in Wiener-Neustadt. (Ibid.)

With his innate interest in the humanities, young Rudolf was naturally inclined to an education in the gymnasium, except that his father wanted him to become a railway civil engineer, and consequently enrolled Steiner in a nearby realschule when he turned eleven.

Later in life, Rudolf Steiner made the startling conjecture that if he had not been educated at the realschule, but had instead attended the gymnasium and been taught by the Cistercian priests there, he would undoubtedly have joined the Order and become a Cistercian priest himself.

I was deeply attracted to all these [Cistercian] priests, many of whom were extremely learned men. I read a great deal that they wrote and was profoundly stirred by it. I loved these priests and the only reason why I passed the Cistercian Order by was because I did not attend the Gymnasium. Karma led me elsewhere. (Lecture given on "The Karma of the Anthroposophical Society," 18 June 1924)

If Rudolf Steiner had become a Cistercian priest, it is unlikely that he would have established anthroposophy—a modern-day expression of *esoteric* Christianity—within the monastic confines of the *exoteric* Catholic Church. Nevertheless, the fact that Rudolf Steiner was willing to become a member of the Cistercian Order clearly indicates that he was not anti-Catholic, or that he considered the Church to be entirely outdated or irrelevant.

Steiner's youthful realization (in the late 1880s) that his esoteric Christian ideas—especially regarding the person of Christ-Jesus and the notion of repeated earth lives—were incompatible with the accepted doctrine of the nineteenth-century Catholic Church, was strengthened and confirmed by his interaction with another respected Cistercian monk, Wilhelm Anton Neumann.

When Steiner knew him, Neumann was professor of Old Testament studies and oriental languages at the University of Vienna. Steiner considered Neumann to be one of the finest representatives of Catholicism; so if Neumann was unable to understand and accept his esoteric Christian ideas, then it was certain that the far-less open-minded Church authorities of the day would not even remotely consider them. As Steiner recalled:

> I expressed my view [to Neumann] that Jesus of Nazareth, through an extra-earthly influence, received the Christ into himself, and that Christ, as a spiritual being, has lived with human evolution since the Mystery of Golgotha. This conversation remains deeply engraved in my soul; it was deeply significant to me and has often surfaced in my memory. The conversation really took place between three individuals—professor Neumann, me, and an invisible third, the personification of Catholic Dogmatism, who appeared to my spiritual eye behind Neumann; it accompanied him, reprovingly tapping his shoulder whenever the scholar's subtle logic led him to agree with me too much. It was remarkable how often the second half of what he was saying would be directly the opposite of the first half. I was face to face with Catholicism as expressed in one of its finest representatives. Through him I learned to respect it, but also to recognize it for what it is [exoteric Christianity?] (*The Course of My Life*; 1986)

2.4 Steiner's Significant Past-Life Connection to Catholicism

Catholicism ran exceedingly deep in Rudolf Steiner's immortal soul, which once again makes it highly unlikely that he could karmically turn his "anthroposophical" back on the Church of St. Peter. As most anthroposophists are well-aware, Rudolf Steiner was previously embodied during the thirteenth century as St. Thomas Aquinas, the foremost "Doctor of the Universal Church."

As well as being the preeminent Scholastic philosopher and theologian of his day, St. Thomas also possessed advanced supersensible perception. On one occasion, Blessed Mary appeared to him and offered assurance that his life and writings were acceptable to God. On another occasion, St. Peter and St. Paul appeared and provided assistance to correctly interpret an obscure passage from the Bible.

St. Thomas also experienced several profound mystical experiences, especially in connection with Holy Communion. In 1273, for example, during one such ecstatic experience in front of the altar, he was witnessed to be levitating, during which a voice issuing from the crucifix declared: "Thou hast written well of me, Thomas; what reward wilt thou have?" St. Thomas is said to have replied, "None other than thyself, Lord."

About four months prior to his death on 7 March 1274, St. Thomas experienced a prolonged ecstatic event during Mass, and later confided to his confessor and companion, Reginald of Piperno: "I can do no more [writing]. Such secrets have been revealed to me that all I have written now appears to be of little value, like straw in the wind." Esoterically understood, St. Thomas was presented with the karmic pre-vision of his next incarnation, and the sublime spiritual truths that he was destined in the future to reveal.

Also in this connection, observant esoteric investigators

will see in the immortalized volumes of St. Thomas' *Summa Theologica* the firmly planted seeds of what would in a later incarnation become anthroposophy—spiritual science. Take, for example, the statement:

> Since the chief aim of this **sacred science** [emphasis added] is to give the knowledge of God, not only as He is in Himself, but also as He is the Beginning of all things, and the End of all, especially of rational creatures, we shall treat first of God; secondly, of the rational creature's advance towards God (*de motu creaturae rationalis in Deum*); thirdly, of Christ, Who, as Man, is the way by which we tend to God."

Also in connection with the events surrounding St. Thomas' death, we gain a clear understanding of why the Cistercians were so karmically-intertwined in the life of Rudolf Steiner. Though St. Thomas was a lifelong member of the Dominican Order (the Order of Preachers, or "Black Friars"), his last days were spent under the devoted care of the Cistercian monks at the Abbey of Fossanova. The pious and humble St. Thomas was deeply moved by the kind attentiveness of the Cistercians to his dying needs, and expressed to Reginald: "This is my rest for ever and ever: here will I dwell, for I have chosen it" (Psalm 131:14).

When the "last rites" were being administered, and St. Thomas was presented with the Eucharistic host—the Sacred Viaticum (Latin: "provisions for the journey")—his enduring connection to the Catholic Faith was clearly evident in his last spoken words:

> If in this world there be any knowledge of this sacrament stronger than that of faith, I wish now to use it in affirming that I firmly believe and know as certain that Jesus Christ, True God and True Man, Son of God and Son of the Virgin Mary, is in this Sacrament ... I receive Thee, the price of my redemption, for Whose love I have

watched, studied, and laboured. Thee have I preached; Thee have I taught. Never have I said anything against Thee: if anything was not well said, that is to be attributed to my ignorance. Neither do I wish to be obstinate in my opinions, but if I have written anything erroneous concerning this sacrament or other matters, I submit all to the judgment and correction of the Holy Roman Church, in whose obedience I now pass from this life.

CHAPTER 3

DID ROMAN CATHOLICISM ABOLISH THE SPIRIT IN 869 AD?

3.1 What Did Rudolf Steiner Mean by "Abolishing the Spirit"?

A RECURRING CRITICISM that Rudolf Steiner leveled at the corrupt and nefarious forces that have acted within Roman Catholicism[4] was that during the Eighth Ecumenical Council of 869 AD, "the spirit was abolished." But since "spirit" is the divine nature of God, there is no way in heaven and earth that it can, in any way, be "abolished." Not even God can abolish his own nature. Besides, why would a powerful, monotheistic religion based on the existence of God as a spiritual being wish to abolish the spirit?

So, then, what could Rudolf Steiner possibly mean when he talks about "abolishing the spirit" in 869? In a lecture given on 6 June 1920, entitled "Roman Catholicism," Steiner has provided some clarification:

> The Catholic Church, by doing away with the spirit in the Eighth Ecumenical Council in Constantinople in the year

869 has always taken care that those belonging to it should never think about the real psycho-spiritual nature of man. The Church laid down in that Council that man consists only of body and soul, though the soul has a few spiritual attributes; but that to regard man as consisting of body, soul and spirit is heretical.

3.2 The Heretical Notion that Human Beings Have Two Souls

In other words, Steiner alleged that what was "abolished" was the religious notion that human nature was a "trichotomy" consisting of body, soul and spirit. Instead, as affirmed by the Council, human nature was a "dichotomy" consisting only of body and soul. While a dogmatic affirmation of dichotomy can certainly be inferred from the wording contained in Canon 11 of the Council, in fact the word "spirit" was not even mentioned in the Canon text, only the notion of "two souls," as the following quotation will attest:

Though the old and new Testament teach that a man or woman has one rational and intellectual soul, and all the fathers and doctors of the church, who are spokesmen of God, express the same opinion, some have descended to such a depth of irreligion, through paying attention to the speculations of evil people, that they shamelessly teach as a dogma that a human being has two souls, and keep trying to prove their heresy by irrational means using a wisdom that has been made foolishness. Therefore this holy and universal synod is hastening to uproot this wicked theory now growing like some loathsome form of weed. Carrying in its hand the winnowing fork of truth, with the intention of consigning all the chaff to inextinguishable fire, and making clean the threshing floor of Christ, in ringing tones it declares anathema the inventors and perpetrators of such impiety and all those holding similar views; it also declares and promulgates that nobody at all should hold or preserve in any way the written teaching of the authors of this impiety. If however anyone presumes to act in a way contrary to this holy and great synod, let him be anathema and an outcast from the faith and way of life of Christians.

Also interesting to note, the theological content of Canon 11 was not discussed or debated by the Council; it was simply accepted (as one of 26 other Canons that were presented at the time). This is not particularly surprising since the Council was especially convened for political, rather than theological reasons; particularly to settle matters of jurisdiction and leadership between the Western and Eastern Churches. That's why the Council was held in Constantinople, and also referred to as "The Fourth Council of Constantinople."

3.3 Understanding the Trichotomy of Body, Soul and Spirit

Rather than the trichotomy of body, soul and spirit, what was actually deemed to be heretical in Canon 11 was the idea that human beings possessed two souls, rather than one. This was a centuries-old Gnostic belief that was still held by some Eastern Christians at the time of the Council. No doubt this persistent notion was based on pre-Christian Greek philosophy (such as Aristotle's) which postulated that there are three different kinds of soul: (1) a vegetative soul, (2) a sensitive soul, and (3) a rational soul. The vegetative soul maintained the functions of nutrition, growth and reproduction; and was possessed by plants, animals and humans. The sensitive soul accounted for feelings, sensation, sensory perception and mobility; and was possessed by the higher animals and humans. The rational soul enabled speech and abstract intellection; and was possessed only by human beings.

It was also understood in Greek philosophy that individual creatures only possessed one soul: plants only possessed a vegetative soul; animals only possessed a sensitive soul—though it also performed the functions of a vegetative soul; and humans beings only possessed a rational soul—though it also performed the functions of a vegetative soul and a sensitive soul. Greek philosophy, then, supported the Council's theological position that human beings do not have more than one soul.

Concerning the trichotomy of human nature into body, soul and spirit, even though there is some distinction of body ("soma"), soul ("psyche") and spirit ("pneuma") in Greek philosophy, the simpler dichotomy of body and soul was much more widely accepted by philosophers. Similarly in ancient Hebrew writing, though there was a distinction of body ("basar"), soul ("nefesh") and spirit ("ruach"), the concept of a trichotomy of human nature was not widely held or theologically embraced.

Nevertheless, in the first three centuries of the Christian era, the trichotomy of human nature was considered orthodox and strongly supported by many church fathers, such as St. Irenaeus, St. Clement of Alexandria, St. Gregory of Nyssa and St. Basil the Great. There are also scriptural passages that clearly indicate that St. Paul supported this idea as well. For example, in 1 Thessalonians 5:23, he stated the following:

> May the God of peace himself sanctify you wholly; and may your spirit and soul and body be kept sound and blameless at the coming of our Lord Jesus Christ.[5]

And in Hebrews 4:12, he makes a clear distinction between the soul and spirit, as indicated from the following:

For the word of God is living and active, sharper than any two-edged sword, piercing to the division of soul and spirit, of joints and marrow, and discerning the thoughts and intentions of the heart.

In the fourth century, hundreds of years prior to the Eighth Ecumenical Council in 869, it was the immense influence of St. Augustine of Hippo (354–430) that really extinguished the notion of human trichotomy as a Catholic belief. In opposing the Semi-Pelagian heresy, St. Augustine held to a dichotomy of human nature, and regarded the differentiation of soul and spirit as an "unprofitable distinction."

In the later Medieval centuries, the dichotomy view of human nature was given additional weighty support in the philosophical writings of St. Thomas Aquinas. In other words, though Rudolf Steiner repeatedly criticized the loss of the trichotomy view of human nature in his twentieth-century lectures, during his incarnation as St. Thomas he actually contributed to its continued extinction in Catholic belief.

3.4 Understanding Human Nature as a Dichotomy of Body and Soul (Together With Some Spiritual Aspects)

Besides that, even according to anthroposophical teachings, the idea that spirit is not a distinct feature of human nature; but rather, is a higher aspect or supernal extension of the soul, is clearly supported as well. The soul element of human nature, according to anthroposophy, is a tripartite fusion of sentient soul, intellectual soul and consciousness soul. The spirit element of human nature is similarly a tripartite fusion of spirit-self, life-spirit and spirit-body (or spirit-man).

As taught in anthroposophy, the spiritual aspect of human nature is nurtured and unfolded by developing and perfecting the human soul. Therefore, perfecting the sentient soul unfolds and develops the spirit-self; perfecting the intellectual soul enlivens the life-spirit; and perfecting the consciousness soul stimulates the growth of spirit-body (refer to Figure 2 below). So even in an anthroposophical sense, then, what is regarded as "spirit" can be alternatively and correctly viewed as "spiritualized soul"; such that human nature can be described as a dichotomy of body and soul (with a spiritualized extension to it).

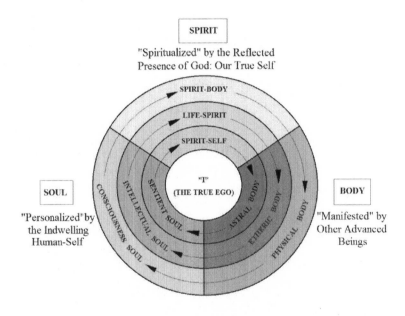

Figure 2: The Anthroposophical Trichotomy

When correctly understood, then, a dichotomy of human

nature into body and soul (together with spiritual attributes) quite accurately corresponds to reality. Moreover, if the term, "spirit," applies exclusively to the divine nature of God, and since human beings are creations, then spirit cannot logically be an independent aspect of human nature. The indivisible spirit of God cannot be divided up and apportioned amongst multiple human beings.

3.5 The Spirit of God Reflected in Each Human Soul

Even though the word, "spirit," most accurately applies only to the divine nature of God (the Creator), and not to human nature (a creation), this does not mean that "spirit is abolished" from human nature. Spirit is an essential aspect of our human constitution; in fact, spirit is what imbues us with life and reality. But correctly understood, a certain quantity or specific amount of spirit has not been apportioned to each human being. Rather, each human soul (which *has* been immortally apportioned to us) has the mirroring capacity to *reflect* the spirit of God within it. This divine reflection is what constitutes our living reality, our real "I," our true self. In this way the spirit of God remains one and indivisible, but also is individualized in each human soul.

What is defined as "spirit" in anthroposophy—spirit-self, life-spirit and spirit-body—is really a tripartite assemblage of higher vehicles of consciousness that better *reflect* the one spirit of God (which constitutes our true self). These elevated vehicles of consciousness are composed of ultra-rarified matter, energy and mind—not spirit. The better they reflect the spirit of God within them, however, the more "spiritualized" they become.

COSMIC REALMS OF EXISTENCE	INDIVIDUAL LEVELS OF EXISTENCE	VEHICLES OF EXPRESSION		SANSKRIT TERMS	DEGREES OF CONSCIOUSNESS
CELESTIAL WORLD [SPIRIT LAND]	SPIRIT	THE HIGHER EGO (SELF)	SPIRIT-BODY	ATMAN	DIVINE CONSCIOUSNESS
			LIFE-SPIRIT	BUDDHI	COSMIC CONSCIOUSNESS
			SPIRIT-SELF	MANAS	SPIRITUAL CONSCIOUSNESS
SOUL WORLD	SOUL	THE LOWER EGO (SELF)	CONSCIOUSNESS SOUL		SOUL CONSCIOUSNESS
			INTELLECTUAL SOUL	KAMA-RUPA	SELF CONSCIOUSNESS
			SENTIENT SOUL		WAKING CONSCIOUSNESS
PHYSICAL WORLD	BODY		ASTRAL BODY	LINGA-SHARIRA	DREAM CONSCIOUSNESS
			ETHERIC BODY	PRANA-JIVA	SLEEP CONSCIOUSNESS
			PHYSICAL BODY	STHULA-SHARIRA	TRANCE CONSCIOUSNESS

Figure 3: Vehicles of Expression and Degrees of Consciousness
According to Anthroposophy

The fully-conscious, first-hand experience of the spirit of God reflected in the human soul as the indwelling "I AM" was actualized and attained for the first time in human history by Christ-Jesus. Prior to his incarnation, the spirit of God as true self, as the "I AM," was experienced externally in the outer world; not internally within the soul. The ancient Hebrew prophet, Moses, for example, experienced the "I AM" spirit of God issuing externally from a burning bush.

In anthroposophical terminology, this internal experience of God reflected in the soul characterizes the developmental level of spirit-self (see Figure 3). The supersensible experience itself is more commonly known as "spirit consciousness" or "real-I consciousness." To anthroposophical understanding, the Graeco-Roman cultural era (747 BC–AD 1413) was destined to develop the intellectual soul. In our current Modern Age era (which will last for about 2160 years), individuals are required to develop the consciousness soul. Consequently, very few individuals have begun to unfold or to actively develop the awareness of spirit-self.

The Catholic Church (as an institution of exoteric Christianity), therefore, cannot be faulted for not including the tripartite human spirit (as revealed by anthroposophy) in its theological teachings during the ninth century (at the time of the Eighth Ecumenical Council). This advanced wisdom-information quite rightly belongs to future human development, and with the greater mysteries of esoteric Christianity (please refer to Figure 3 for diagrammatical clarification).

3.6 Corrupt "Initiates" Within the Medieval Church Exploit the Dichotomy for Power and Control

While a comprehensive, esoteric understanding of the trichotomy of human nature was too advanced for most

Medieval theologians in 896 AD, there were some who had surreptitiously obtained partial knowledge of "the spirit within human nature." These "illicit initiates" militantly embraced a distorted vision of Christianity where the Church in Rome had complete control of world religion through a centralized priesthood that acted as the sole mediators between ordinary humanity and the spiritual world. If more and more people came to realize that it was possible to experience the spirit of God reflected in their own soul, then the Roman Church (as they distortedly envisioned it) would lose monopoly control over people's religious lives.

Therefore, as Rudolf Steiner has repeatedly indicated, beginning with the Eighth Ecumenical Council, this small but influential cabal of corrupt and power-hungry Churchmen has worked fanatically to suppress any consideration of the trichotomy or any knowledge of the indwelling spirit. It was these corrupt, Medieval Church officials (and their successors)—*not* the Catholic Church as established by Christ-Jesus—who fought to "abolish the personal experience of the indwelling spirit" in people's soul lives.

3.7 The Inner Experience of the Spirit Now Encouraged by the Catholic Church

The subversive activity throughout the centuries to suppress the inner experience of the spirit was clearly anti-Christian and runs completely contrary to the incarnational mission of Christ-Jesus. Thankfully today, even though the Catholic Church still theologically maintains the dichotomy of human nature, it likewise actively encourages and promotes the inner experience of the spirit.

In the sacrament of baptism, for example, the stain of original sin upon the soul and body is washed away by the heavenly descent and inmost penetration of the Holy Spirit of

God. Thereby, the baptized Christian becomes a living "temple of the spirit"; a redeemed neophyte of body, soul and spirit.

Moreover, as a temple of the Holy Spirit, the human heart is now considered to be the "new tabernacle," and the soul is now considered to be the living "holy of holies" wherein dwells the spirit of God.

Furthermore, in the sacrament of Holy Communion, by ingesting the consecrated bread and wine, it is understood that the "Real Presence" of the Risen Saviour (body, blood, soul and divinity of Christ-Jesus) is received internally—the soul of the recipient unites with the spirit (divinity) of Christ-Jesus.

Even in the newly-revised translation of the Mass (instituted in 2011), the greeting of the priest-celebrant: "The Lord be with you," is now responded to by the congregation with: "And with your spirit."

From these examples, it is reasonable to conclude that the Catholic Church of today very much "embraces the personal experience of the indwelling spirit." Those nefarious factions within the Church that have historically striven to abolish this experience have finally been silenced.

CHAPTER 4

THE POWER AND INFLUENCE OF JESUITISM WITHIN THE CATHOLIC CHURCH

4.1 A Brief History of the Jesuit Order

FEW (IF ANY) HISTORIANS would deny that the Society of Jesus—the Jesuits—have had a colourful and controversial past. Over the centuries, the Jesuit Order has been celebrated and condemned; welcomed and banished; respected and vilified; honoured and afflicted. Jesuits have been advisors and confidants to kings and mandarins, as well as ignominious missionaries in savage, wilderness regions of the globe. Jesuits have risen to heights of greatness and achievement; and fallen to depths of depravity and disrepute. Clearly, this is a Catholic organization worth noting and examining.

From the very beginning, the Jesuit Order was characterized by a fervent and strong-willed militancy—not surprising since it was founded by a zealous and ambitious professional soldier, Ignatius of Loyola (c.1491–1556), who had been forced to give up military life because of a serious cannon ball injury to both his legs. As a result, he transferred his military zeal and ambition to the spiritual life. In 1534, when St. Ignatius and six companions dedicated themselves in Paris to establishing a new Catholic order, it was no surprise that the opening lines of the founding document declared that the Society was founded for "whoever desires to serve as a soldier of God." Since then, the Jesuits have come to be known as "God's Soldiers," "God's Marines" and "the Pope's Secret Service."

St. Ignatius also incorporated an element of strict military obedience into the Society, by requiring of members a separate vow of unquestioning obedience to the pope (in addition to the usual vows of poverty, chastity and obedience). Consequently, Jesuits have also been referred to as "the Pope's Men." In one of the 18 *Rules for Thinking with the Church*, St. Ignatius famously described the Jesuit vow of absolute obedience as follows:

> That we may be altogether of the same mind and in conformity with the [pope and] Church herself, if she shall have defined anything to be black which to our eyes appears to be white, we ought in like manner to pronounce it to be black.

In order to properly train and prepare prospective Jesuits, St. Ignatius formulated his well-known *Spiritual Exercises*, a series of intense and vivid meditations and visualizations that are conducted over a four-week period. The *Spiritual Exercises* are intended as a "call to action," as an incitement to religious militancy by strengthening the will-resolve to become a dedicated foot-soldier in the army of Jesus.

From the very beginning, Jesuit education and training has emphasized academic excellence and attainment, in addition to the basic *Spiritual Exercises*. The Jesuit formation for the priesthood normally takes eight to fourteen years of classical studies and theology to complete. Consequently, Jesuits have been historically known to be highly educated and very well-informed. Not surprisingly, then, they quickly rose to become trusted advisors and scholastic tutors to the wealthy and powerful dynasties of Europe. Unfortunately, because of these influential connections, unscrupulous Jesuits also became involved in political intrigues, state espionage, military agitation, subversive activity—even in assassinations and plots to overthrow the ruling elites.

Throughout most of their 450 year history, the Jesuit Order has been regarded as an ultra-orthodox, ultra-conservative force within the Catholic Church. Not surprisingly, then, the Jesuit Order played a major role in the Counter-Reformation movement—the opposition of the Catholic Church to the growing influence of Protestantism throughout Europe—which lasted from 1545 until 1648. The Jesuits were instrumental in re-converting a number of European countries that had become Protestant, notably Poland and Lithuania.

The emphasis on educational attainment, together with the directive to evangelize and promote the Catholic Faith, has resulted in the Jesuit establishment of numerous schools, colleges, seminaries and universities throughout the world. Even today, the Jesuit Order is educationally active in 112 countries on six different continents. Since Jesuit schools have traditionally included the study of vernacular (non-Latin) literature and rhetoric (the art of discourse, speech-making and persuasion), certain institutions (such as Georgetown University in Washington, DC) have become important training centres for lawyers, judges, politicians, government bureaucrats and public officials.[6]

4.2   Rudolf Steiner and "Jesuitism"

Of all the criticism that Rudolf Steiner directed at Catholicism, his harshest comments were aimed at what he termed, "Jesuitism." It is important to understand that Steiner's criticism of Jesuitism is not a blanket criticism of the entire Jesuit Order, or of any particular Jesuit. Concerning individual members of the Order, Steiner readily acknowledged that throughout history there have been outstanding Jesuit geniuses that are little known because they self-effacingly avoided fame and recognition as humble servants of their Order. As expressed in a lecture given on 6 June 1920, entitled "Roman Catholicism":

> On the subject of the Jesuits ... There are numerous men within the Order of such spiritual capacity that if they were scattered about the world and did not spend their time in the way they do but were working at external science or painting or poetry, they would be honored as individual geniuses; they would be recognized as the great minds of mankind. Within the Jesuit Order there are countless men who would be great lights if they were to appear as individuals and were busy with something different—with, for instance, materialistic science. But these men suppress their names; they submerge themselves within their Order.

Correctly speaking, with "Jesuitism," what Steiner is referring to is the extremist ideological attitude that grants unquestioning allegiance to external authority and autocratic stricture; and which views the world in polarized, absolutist terms of "black and white," "good and evil," "us and them." What Steiner called "Jesuitism" is today better referred to as "fundamentalism." For modern-day thinking, much of Steiner's references to "Jesuitism" is better understood if the word, "fundamentalism," or "fundamentalist," is substituted in its place. Take, for example, the following quotation where this has been done:

And in the age which prompted by modern life feels the first stirrings of a need to think freely, we find the opposing power at work in the so-called Jesuitism [fundamentalism] of the different religions—although much comes under this heading which would have to be described in detail ...

In our time putting faith in authority has become so great and so intensified that under its influence people are losing their power of judgment ... We are becoming bound hand and foot to our belief in authority ... above all we must realize that we have increasingly to contend with our own trust in authority, and that whole theories are being built up which in their turn will become the basis of convictions only serving to uphold belief in authority.

In medicine, in law and in every other sphere people declare themselves from the outset incompetent to judge, and accept what science tells them. The complications of modern life make this understandable. But under the pressure of authority we shall become more and more helpless. And systematically to build up this force of authority, this habit of authority, is actually *the principle of Jesuitism* [fundamentalism]. And Jesuitism [fundamentalism] in the Catholic religion ... begins in the sphere of ecclesiastical dogma with the tendency to uphold papal authority projected over from the fourth post-Atlantean period into the fifth where it can do no good. But the same Jesuitical [fundamentalist] principle will gradually transfer itself to other spheres of life. In a form hardly differing from the Jesuitism [fundamentalism] of dogmatic religion, we already find it in medical circles where a certain dogmatism strives after more power for the medical profession. This is typical of Jesuitical [fundamentalist] aspiration everywhere; and it will grow stronger and stronger. People will find

35

themselves more and more tied down by what authority imposes upon them. And in face of this ahrimanic opposition—for such it is—salvation for the fifth post-Atlantean epoch will be found in asserting the rights of the consciousness soul which is wishing to develop. (From a lecture given on 10 October 1916 entitled, "How Can the Destitution of Soul in Modern Times be Overcome?")

By doing this word substitution, Rudolf Steiner's statements become eerily prophetic: fundamentalism (Jesuitism) is indeed one of the great scourges of our day. As well as the radical Islamic fundamentalism that is currently terrorizing the entire Middle East, there is the right-wing Christian fundamentalism that is polarizing and distorting American politics, religion, legislation and culture. Steiner is prognostically exact in describing how the vast majority of persons today fail to think for themselves, thereby relying entirely on "expert authority" in all aspects of life: science, medicine, economics, politics, law, art and technology. Today, "blind faith in authority" is much more common *outside* of religion, than it is *within* faith-institutions such as the Catholic Church.

4.3   Jesuit Initiation versus Rosicrucian Initiation

Aside from the strict religious fundamentalism that has long been cultivated within the Order, the second major concern that Rudolf Steiner had with the Jesuits was the Ignatian *Spiritual Exercises* that were (and still are) employed for faith-formation. To the casual observer, however, this training appears innocuous enough: it is basically a month-long, four-step process of prayer, meditation and contemplation. Each of the four weeks of training focuses on a different meditative theme:

Week 1: focuses on human sin
Week 2: focuses on Christ-Jesus' life on earth
Week 3: focuses on the Saviour's death on the cross
Week 4: focuses on the Redeemer's risen life

Except in a couple of instances, meditative imagery is taken from the New Testament. Similar to the Benedictine practice of "Lectio Divina," the Jesuit aspirant is instructed to creatively visualize these biblical scenes as realistically as possible, and then to imaginatively enter into these visualizations. By doing so, it is intended that one's will-resolve is aroused and directed into becoming a committed "soldier of God in the army of Jesus." While the end result of the *Spiritual Exercises* certainly smacks of religious fundamentalism (reminding one of the current Muslim jihadists who fanatically see themselves as "soldiers of God in the army of Mohammad"), for most participants and observers the meditative exercises themselves raise no particular alarm bells of concern.[7]

To the sensitive clairvoyant perception of Rudolf Steiner, however, the *Spiritual Exercises* were seen to employ some potentially dangerous methods of occult initiation. This is not to say that individual Jesuits have been aware of this, or that St. Ignatius consciously established or intended this. Rather than being the result of human invention, Steiner has indicated that the harmful occult elements contained in the *Spiritual Exercises* were inspired by dark spiritual forces; that is, by Ahriman (Satan) and Lucifer.

As a Rosicrucian initiate, one of the major occult concerns that Rudolf Steiner had with the Ignatian *Spiritual Exercises* was that they are purposely intended to directly affect the human will. In Rosicrucian spiritual training (initiation), however, the human will is considered sacrosanct and inviolable. As such, Rosicrucian initiation only concentrates on developing human thinking, thereby leaving the application of one's individual will, free and unaffected.

As well as targeting the human will, during the second week of the *Spiritual Exercises*, two very powerful meditative visualizations that are not taken from the New Testament are also included. The first of these is entitled, "The Call of the Temporal King." With this visualization, Christ-Jesus is to be vividly imagined as a military-style, temporal king whose will is "to conquer all the world and all enemies and so enter into the glory of [God the] Father." The second visualization is entitled, "Meditation on Two Standards," and vividly imagines Christ-Jesus as the military general of an immense army that is preparing to do battle with an equally immense army led by Lucifer. In the words of St. Ignatius:

> It will be here to see a great field of all that region of Jerusalem, where the supreme Commander-in-chief of the good is Christ our Lord; another field in the region of Babylon, where the chief of the enemy is Lucifer.

Even for those Christians who do not possess Rudolf Steiner's extensive clairvoyant ability, these two visualizations disturbingly contradict the non-violent image of Christ-Jesus as the "Lord of Love," who instructed mankind to "Love your enemies, do good to those who hate you" (Luke 6:27); to not strike back in revenge, but "If anyone slaps you on the right cheek, turn to them the other cheek also" (Matt 5:39); and who declared, "My kingship is not of this world; if my kingship were of this world, my servants would fight" (Jn 18:36).

Furthermore, these two visualizations are also disturbingly similar to the Wilderness temptation that Christ-Jesus rejected, that would have Luciferically placed him as the temporal ruler over all the kingdoms and armies of the earth. Clearly these two Ignatian visualizations distort and contradict the true Christ-Jesus; and instead, substitute and glorify a worldly, militaristic Antichrist.

The strength and influence of these two infernally-inspired

visualizations is, of course, dependent on how vividly and realistically they are imagined, how deeply they are entered into, and how powerfully they activate the candidate's own will-power to act. These three conditions largely account for the historical fact that the great majority of Jesuits, who have sincerely undertaken the *Spiritual Exercises*, are not detrimentally or seriously affected by them. Likewise, it does explain why certain Jesuits, throughout the history of the Order, have been fanatically driven to establish a militaristic, dictatorial-style "Catholicism" as the dominantly-exclusive world-religion.

4.4   Fanatical Jesuits and Freemasonry

While there was certainly significant and fundamental differences between Jesuit and Rosicrucian spiritual training (initiation), there has been a much more rancorous relationship between Jesuits and Freemasons. No doubt this was due to the fact that Freemasonry (unlike Rosicrucianism) has been a widespread and powerful secret society that has included presidents, kings, prime ministers, noblemen, aristocrats, statesmen, judges, bankers and military-generals among its historical ranks.

Though Freemasonry pays lip-service to God as "The Great Architect of the Universe" (TGAOTU), "Speculative" Freemasonry is essentially a hollowed-out remnant of the ancient pagan Mystery religions. Ironically, Freemasonry began as a medieval guild of practicing stonemasons ("Operative" Freemasons) who were devoted to the Roman Catholic Church. Unfortunately, as the medieval stone construction of castles, fortresses and cathedrals slowly disappeared, the guarded guild-houses of practicing stonemasons gradually morphed into the secretive lodges of non-practicing "Speculative Masons."

Though historically there have been multiple and sometimes conflicting forms of Freemasonry, one shared ideal has been the establishment of a world-wide, secular utopian state, a "New World Order," that is more egalitarian and free from any religious constraint. Not surprisingly, then, Freemasons were influential agitators and participants in the French and American Revolutions. As strong proponents of, and influential activists for, the strict separation of church and state, Freemasons have oftentimes been vehemently anti-Catholic; and have thereby incurred the reciprocal hostility of fundamentalist Jesuits.

Beginning in 1738, the Catholic Church (and other major denominations) repeatedly condemned Freemasonry as being incompatible and irreconcilable with Christianity. As such, Catholics were prohibited (even to this day) from becoming Freemasons. As recent as 1983, the Church has declared:

> [T]he Church's negative judgment in regard to Masonic associations remains unchanged since their principles have always been considered irreconcilable with the doctrine of the Church and, therefore, membership in them remains forbidden. The faithful, who enroll in Masonic associations are in a state of grave sin and may not receive Holy Communion.

Obviously, this longstanding Church prohibition on Catholics becoming Freemasons stringently applies also to members of the Jesuit Order. Therefore, it comes as a bit of a shock and surprise to learn from Rudolf Steiner that, during his time (beginning in 1802), there was a secret cooperation between Jesuits and Freemasons for world domination: the Jesuits would control world-religion; and the Anglo-American Freemasonic lodges would control world finance and government. As one example, in a lecture given on 4 April 1916 entitled, "Secrets of Freemasonry," Steiner stated:

> You know that the Jesuits battle against the Freemasons

and vice versa. However, the upper orders of the Freemasons and the upper orders of the Jesuits build a special brotherhood; they build a state within a state.

Such an unlikely collusion appears wildly conspiratorial at first, and is exceedingly difficult to substantiate without clairvoyant perception or "insider" information. On further reflection, however, the idea that prominent Jesuits had (during Steiner's time) infiltrated the upper echelons of Freemasonry, in the same way that Freemasons have covertly penetrated the Vatican, is not entirely untenable. Even if there was no actual collusion, as powerful ideological opponents, both sides would certainly have had a strong vested interest in spying on the other. Furthermore, if there was a covert conspiracy involving Jesuits and Freemasons (as Steiner has indicated), these would have been heretical, renegade Jesuits that were acting *in defiance* of the Catholic Church—not *in obedience* to canon law. No doubt such covert activity was kept well-hidden from the Catholic authorities of the day, and from their own Jesuit overseers; both of which would certainly have strongly condemned such criminal activity.

4.5   Renegade Jesuits as Communist Sympathizers

Those familiar with Rudolf Steiner's numerous critical comments on reactionary Jesuits will undoubtedly be astonished to learn that the dissident Jesuits of the twentieth century were diametrically different—180 degrees different—than the rogue Jesuits of prior centuries. Whereas the original Jesuits of the sixteenth and seventeenth centuries declared war on Lucifer and his army; and the Jesuits of the eighteenth and nineteenth centuries declared war on Freemasonry and the secret "Anglo-American Lodges"; the radical Jesuits of the twentieth century declared war on the capitalist system.

Without question, the renegade Jesuits of Steiner's day were radically right-wing, ultra-orthodox, and fanatically fundamentalist. The renegade Jesuits of the mid-to-late twentieth century, however, were radically left-wing, ultra-heterodox, and rabidly communist. As such, few of the Jesuit criticisms that Rudolf Steiner made during his day can be accurately applied to the radical Jesuits of today.

Beginning soon after the Second World War, certain intellectual and socially-conscious Jesuits (as well as other Catholic priests) began to formulate a heterodox theology that focused on alleviating poverty and the unjust oppression of the poor—particularly in Latin America. Much of the philosophical foundation of this radical theology was based on Marxist ideology, and was therefore a kind of "Christianized communism" or "communist Christianity." After the publication in 1971 of the declarative and influential book, *A Theology of Liberation*, by Peruvian priest Gustavo Gutierrez, this Marxist theology became better known as "liberation theology."

Not surprisingly, due to its communist underpinnings, liberation theology was a clarion call to world-wide social activism, radical upheaval, class conflict and even armed revolution. Rather than being a Church-approved "theology of salvation," liberation theology was actually a Church-condemned "theology of revolution." During the 1970s and 80s, for example, Jesuit priests and theologians became actively involved in the violent, armed revolution in Nicaragua. One particular Jesuit, Fernando Cardenal (b.1934), served as minister of education from 1984 to 1990 in the communist Sandinista government of Nicaragua.

Throughout the tenure of Pope John Paul II (1978–2005), then, liberation theology Jesuits were openly hostile and publically defiant of papal authority. They were hardly the ultra-obedient, "corpse-like" servants of the pope and the

Roman Church that St. Ignatius had envisioned, and that Rudolf Steiner repeatedly described. In fact, Jesuit disobedience had degenerated to such a degree that rather than dissolve the Order, Pope John Paul II in 1981 decided to assume temporary control of the Jesuits by appointing a trusted papal representative, Paolo Dezza SJ, to provide a "more thorough preparation" before Jesuits were next permitted to elect their own leader (superior-general).

Concerning communism, the Catholic Church, as succinctly stated in Paragraph 2425 of the *Catechism of the Catholic Church*, officially denounces this atheistic ideology:

> The Church has rejected the totalitarian and atheistic ideologies associated in modem times with "communism" or "socialism." She has likewise refused to accept, in the practice of "capitalism," individualism and the absolute primacy of the law of the marketplace over human labor. Regulating the economy solely by centralized planning perverts the basis of social bonds; regulating it solely by the law of the marketplace fails social justice, for "there are many human needs which cannot be satisfied by the market." Reasonable regulation of the marketplace and economic initiatives, in keeping with a just hierarchy of values and a view to the common good, is to be commended.

Modern-day Jesuits who embrace, promote and practice liberation theology are, therefore, "defiants" and not "defendants" of Catholic orthodoxy. Furthermore, rather than blindly upholding the "top-down," centrally-based, hierarchical leadership of the Church, liberation theologists actively promote a "bottom-up," community-based, communal-style "people's church," a "church of the proletariat (workers)." Once again, this hardly describes the fundamentalist Jesuits of Rudolf Steiner's day.

So for anti-Catholic, anthroposophical critics (such as

Sergei O. Prokofieff: 1954–2014), to rail against the Jesuits of today as if they remained exactly the same as the Jesuits of Rudolf Steiner's day, clearly indicates that these critics haven't bothered to keep up with the times. It's no wonder that Prokofieff engendered the hostility of certain contemporary Jesuits when he was still alive; they were merely defending themselves against his anachronistic and outdated vitriol.

In order to positively bridge the gap between anthroposophists and Jesuits today, it's necessary for each side to be assured that the other side isn't intent on their destruction. In today's social climate, it's safe to say that modern-day Jesuits (even the heterodox ones) are not intent on stamping out world-wide anthroposophy. And reciprocally, most anthroposophists do not share Prokofieff's anti-Catholicism and are certainly not intent on tearing down the universal Catholic Church.

Even if there still exists the odd covert fanatic within each camp, they are increasingly isolated, ineffectual and denounced. In the final analysis, whatever the hostile past, and whatever the uncertain future, Christ-Jesus, the divine source of both exoteric *and* esoteric Christianity, will certainly not allow either of his two mystery-wisdom streams to disappear from the face of the earth.

CHAPTER 5

THE CATHOLIC CONVERSION OF ANTHROPOSOPHIST, VALENTIN TOMBERG

5.1 Who the Heck was "Valentin Tomberg"?

VALENTIN TOMBERG (1900—1973), for much of his adult life, was a contradictory and controversial character. As a young teenager in St. Petersburg, Tomberg was irresistibly drawn to the mystical and the magical; and by the age of seventeen, he was already initiated into the pseudo-Hermetic mysticism of prominent Russian Freemason, Gregory O. Mebes.

When Tomberg was twenty-five and living in Estonia, he became an ardent and active member of the Anthroposophical Society. By the age of thirty, he began to write and lecture on various anthroposophical themes. His unique and original (but often fanciful) ideas very soon attracted wide attention, as well as strong anthroposophical denouncement. From the very beginning, Tomberg viewed anthroposophy through the distorted lens of his dubious pseudo-Hermetic background. Contrary to seeing anthroposophy as a "spiritual science," he distortedly viewed it as an "elevated theory" that leads to the "mysticism and magic of thinking." In Tomberg's own words:

> Rudolf Steiner's Anthroposophy is ... neither just a philosophy which leads over into mysticism, nor just a theory which leads over into magic. It is rather a way to an experience of the spirit world which is as real as the Vedantic experience, yet is as *objective* as are the spiritual phenomena brought down into the material realm by the Western magician. The two paths which proceed out of theory—one into mysticism and the other into magic—are here *not* pursued; but theory itself, or more correctly *thinking*, is lifted up onto a higher level. Anthroposophy thereby becomes *the mysticism and magic of thinking*. (From an essay entitled, "Western Occultism, Vedanta and Anthroposophy"; 1930)

In 1938, as a result of his unsubstantiated and eccentric occult pronouncements and interpretations, Tomberg was "persuaded" to move his family from Estonia to Amsterdam. But only two years later, he decided to withdraw from the Anthroposophical Society in the Netherlands as well. Rather astoundingly, even though he was active in the Dutch anti-Nazi resistance, in 1944 Tomberg moved to Cologne, Germany, where he enrolled in the university there. Then around 1945, he converted to the Roman Catholic Church, and immediately began adapting his quirky Hermeticism to Church doctrine, history and notable religious figures.

5.2   Tomberg's Radical Leap into Fundamentalist Jesuitism

Aside from some controversial esoteric writings, why is it that the life of Valentin Tomberg stirs up such heated debate amongst anthroposophists and Catholics, even today? One plausible esoteric explanation is that because of his lifelong preoccupation with the dubious Hermetic magic of occultists, Gérard Encausse (aka: "Papus": 1865–1916) and Alphonse Louis Constant (aka: "Eliphas Lévi": 1810–1875), together with his vainglorious ambition to become a famous occult teacher,[8] Tomberg unknowingly became a public conduit for influentially-powerful but shadowy superphysical forces and beings. As an anthroposophical teacher and leader, by establishing a "magical," hypno-suggestive hold on participants, Tomberg managed to acquire a retinue of "loyal" followers.

In spite of having no developed supersensible ability (he clearly had no access to the akashic records; nor was he a student or member of the Great White Brotherhood; nor could he consciously converse with highly-advanced celestial beings), Tomberg still arrogantly claimed to be the reincarnated William of Orange, as well as Johann von Goethe. When in Dornach, Switzerland, Tomberg even imperiously attempted to be acknowledged as Rudolf Steiner's anthroposophical successor!

Needless to say, when Tomberg completely turned his back on 21 years of anthroposophical study and involvement to suddenly join the Roman Catholic Church, many of his "star-struck" followers felt callously abandoned and betrayed. Moreover, it's not that Tomberg just quietly became Catholic while still remaining an anthroposophist, he completely severed all acknowledgement and connection with his anthroposophical past. Later in life, he even treated his extensive experience as an anthroposophist as if it were a separate incarnation. In a letter written on 9 March 1970 Tomberg stated:

> [Y]ou will not encounter the [anthroposophical] Valentin Tomberg of the thirties. The distance which separates me from him today is as big as two incarnations. Really I

should now have a different name; but for civil reasons that is not possible. Nothing lies further from me today or would be more tiring than to see the ashes of the anthroposophical past raised up.

Furthermore, upon his zealous Catholic conversion, it's not that Tomberg simply practiced a private, prayerful worship within the Church, he unabashedly embraced "all things Jesuit," publically condemned "all things anthroposophical," and quickly proceeded to intellectually formulate a "Christian Hermeticism." While Tomberg's radical about-face from anthroposophy to Catholicism may appear puzzling at first, it is actually an unvarnished example of his extremist personality. With extremist individuals such as Valentin Tomberg, it is easy to replace one fanatical ideology with another. The point is, whatever they choose to do, extremist personalities will always take it to a fanatical degree. Religious fundamentalists have been known to become hardened atheists, and vice versa. Arch-conservatives have suddenly become left-wing socialists, and vice versa.[9]

Tomberg, then, didn't just convert to traditional, mainstream Catholicism; but instead, fervently embraced the fundamentalist form of Jesuitism that Rudolf Steiner had been repeatedly warning anthroposophists about. By doing so, however, Tomberg was able to retain and promulgate his heretical Hermetic beliefs in magic and Tarot-occultism without attracting the hostile attention of conservative-minded Catholic authorities.

Moreover, during the time that Tomberg converted to Catholicism (around 1945), Jesuit and other clerical renegades had started to become heretically "anti-conservative." As well as challenging the traditional authority, doctrines, and hierarchical structure of the Church, the "ultra-liberal" theologians of the 1960s pressed for "change," and the "need to modernize" the existing Church. Their dominant influence during that time resulted in the sweeping and controversial changes of the Second Vatican Council (1962–1965). In the permissive climate of post-Vatican II, many ultra-liberal theologians (including Jesuits) began to intellectually toy with popular notions of "New Age" spirituality, including Tomberg's personal brand of Hermetic occultism.

5.3   Tomberg and "Hermeticized" Catholicism

After he retired to Reading, England, in 1960, Tomberg began work on his magnum opus of "Hermeticized" Catholicism entitled (in English), *Meditations on the Tarot: A Journey into Christian Hermeticism.* The detailed and extensive work was originally written in French, and took about eleven years to complete. Echoing the eccentric contents of the book, Tomberg chose not to divulge his name as author, and to have the book published anonymously after his death. However, a German translation was published and circulated in 1972 (a year before Tomberg's death) by his best friend and disciple, Ernst von Hippel. Moreover, it was easily established who the "anonymous" author was.

Even a cursory examination of *Meditations on the Tarot,* then, reveals it to be drenched in duplicity and artifice from cover to cover. Why insist on anonymous authorship when the sole reason it has been repeatedly published and "praised" is because Tomberg is the author? On the front cover of the 2002 Penguin publication, why refer to controversial (some would say, heretical)[10] Catholic theologian, Hans Urs von Balthasar (1905–1988) as "Cardinal" when he died before the mandatory papal consistory. The consistory is the formal meeting of the College of Cardinals called by the pope to publish the decree of elevation to the cardinalate. If the pope or the candidate dies before the consistory, as did von Balthasar, all the prior papal nominations are voided.

Furthermore, in the Foreword of the book, why does

Tomberg conclude with, "Your friend greets you, dear Unknown Friend, from beyond the grave," when Tomberg obviously wrote the book while he was still alive, and initially published it a year *before* he died? And why was it important for Tomberg to even want to converse with his readership "from beyond the grave," as if he were psychically conveying the book's contents as a disembodied spirit? Isn't this kind of creepy for a book author to prearrange. On the back cover of the 2002 Penguin publication, it's explained that:

> [T]he intention of this work is for the reader to find a relationship with the author in the spiritual dimensions of existence ... as a friend who is communicating with us from beyond the boundaries of ordinary life.

Doesn't the Catholic Church frown on this kind of "spiritism"? According to Paragraph 2117 of the *Catechism of the Catholic Church*: "Spiritism often implies divination or magical practices; the Church for her part warns the faithful against it."

Also in this connection, on the back cover of this particular publication, a number of Catholic clergymen—Trappist Abbot Basil Pennington, Father Bede Griffiths and Trappist Abbot Thomas Keating—are all ebullient in their praise about a New Age-style book celebrating the Tarot, a deck of cards used primarily for "divination" (fortune telling)! And if that isn't bizarre enough, Catholic theologian von Balthazar begins his Afterword at the back of the book with:

> A thinking, praying Christian of unmistakable purity [Tomberg???] reveals to us the symbols of Christian Hermeticism in its various levels of mysticism, gnosis and magic, taking in also the Cabbala and certain elements of astrology and alchemy.

Here we have, in writing, a "prominent" Catholic theologian embracing and extolling numerous occult practices that the

Catholic Church has long condemned as incompatible with true Christianity. As stated in Paragraph 2116 of the *Catechism of the Catholic Church*:

> All forms of *divination* are to be rejected ... practices falsely supposed to "unveil" the future. Consulting horoscopes, astrology, palm reading, interpretation of omens and lots ... all conceal a desire for power over time, history, and, in the last analysis, other human beings, as well as a wish to conciliate hidden powers. They contradict the honor, respect, and loving fear that we owe to God alone.

And in Paragraph 2117:

> All practices of *magic* or *sorcery*, by which one attempts to tame occult powers, so as to place them at one's service and have a supernatural power over others—even if this were for the sake of restoring their health—are gravely contrary to the virtue of religion. (Ibid.)

Clearly what Tomberg and his contemporary, heterodox Catholic supporters intend with the *Meditations on the Tarot* is for the book to act as a literary "Trojan horse"; that is, as a covert, "under(book)cover" means to surreptitiously slip New Age-style ideology into approved Catholic theology. A 90-page document issued by the Vatican in 2003 entitled, "Jesus Christ, the bearer of the water of life—A Christian reflection on the "New Age," clarifies the Church's position on New Age ideology:

> Even if it can be admitted that *New Age* religiosity in some way responds to the legitimate spiritual longing of human nature, it must be acknowledged that its attempts to do so run counter to Christian revelation. In Western culture in particular, the appeal of "alternative" approaches to spirituality is very strong ...
> At the same time there is increasing nostalgia and

curiosity for the wisdom and ritual of long ago, which is one of the reasons for the remarkable growth in the popularity of esotericism and gnosticism ...

An adequate Christian discernment of *New Age* thought and practice cannot fail to recognize that, like second and third century gnosticism, it represents something of a compendium of positions that the Church has identified as heterodox. John Paul II warns with regard to the "return of ancient gnostic ideas under the guise of the so-called *New Age*: We cannot delude ourselves that this will lead toward a renewal of religion. It is only a new way of practising gnosticism."

By carefully implanting the *Meditations on the Tarot* into the unsuspecting body of Catholic literature, Tomberg's Catholic supporters clearly envision that this "Christian Hermeticism" will attract those interested in New Age occultism into the Church fold.

While Tomberg and his followers acknowledge the existence of "esoteric Christianity" (as in anthroposophy) and "exoteric Christianity" (the Church of St. Peter), they don't regard these two streams as independent, complementary paths. Tombergians believe that all forms of esoteric Christianity (especially anthroposophy) must be placed under the authority of the pope and the hierarchy of the Roman Catholic Church. As Tomberg dogmatically declared in *Meditations on the Tarot*: "Esoteric Christianity lives completely within exoteric Christianity, it does not and cannot exist in separation from it."

Tomberg's statement, of course, is quite preposterous since historical expressions of esoteric Christianity, such as the Knighthood of the Holy Grail, the Fraternity of the Rose Cross and anthroposophy, have all separately existed outside the authoritative umbrella of the Catholic Church. Moreover, throughout the centuries, corrupt officials within the Catholic Church deliberately excluded these expressions of esoteric

Christianity and violently strove to stamp them out—rather than to warmly include them.

This statement also indicates how little Tomberg understood anthroposophy, even after 21 years of intense involvement. Clearly, instead of pretending to be a great anthroposophical teacher, he should have been content to be a sincere anthroposophical student. Since anthroposophy is a science (albeit a spiritual one with a Christocentric focus), to declare that spiritual science can only exist within the confines of the Catholic Church is like saying that biology, chemistry or physics can only exist within the Church. As Steiner repeatedly maintained—anthroposophy is not a religion. As such, it needs to remain separate and apart from religious stricture and authority.

What Tomberg's statement does indicate, however, is that within the current Church of St. Peter, there is a small faction of heterodox clerics and laymen who mistakenly wish to combine esoteric and exoteric Christianity into a "liberalized" form of syncretistic Catholicism.

5.4 *Meditations on the Tarot*: A Journey into Shadowy Occult Deception

Even though, as an anthroposophist, Tomberg was rebuffed in his efforts to be recognized as the esoteric Christian successor to Rudolf Steiner, he still fervently held on to this vainglorious, egocentric delusion throughout his Catholic conversion. His unabashed praise of St. Ignatius and his *Spiritual Exercises* was a subtle contrivance needed to position himself (and the Hermetic "spiritual exercises" of his *Tarot* book) as the Christian successor to St. Ignatius (and thereby, to Rudolf Steiner). What Tomberg had failed to accomplish as an anthroposophist, he was certain he had accomplished as a Catholic esotericist (even "from beyond the grave").

It's perfectly obvious to any sincere esoteric Christian (without a hidden agenda) that Valentin Tomberg cannot hold a candle-flame to the sun-burst of supersensible knowledge issuing from Rosicrucian initiate and "master of wisdom," Rudolf Steiner. Tomberg's feeble attempt with *Meditations on the Tarot* is pathetically obvious.

To begin with, the meditative imagery that Tomberg chooses for his "spiritual exercises" are coloured woodcut designs from Jean Dodal's early eighteenth-century version of the Tarot de Marseille, a deck of cards purportedly invented in the fifteenth century in northern Italy. So why does Tomberg refer to these images as "Hermetic"? According to some occult historians, tarot cards (particularly the major arcana) were originally derived from the ancient Egyptian "Book of Thoth," and later introduced into Medieval Europe by migratory gypsies. As explained by occultist, Manley P. Hall (1901–1990) in *The Secret Teachings of All Ages* (1928):

> A curious legend relates that after the destruction of the Serapeum in Alexandria, the large body of attendant priests banded themselves together to preserve the secrets of the rites of Serapis. Their descendants (Gypsies) carrying with them the most precious of the volumes saved from the burning library—the Book of Enoch, or Thoth (the Tarot)—became wanderers upon the face of the earth, remaining a people apart with an ancient language and a birthright of magic and mystery.

Since the Egyptian god, Thoth, is also known as "Hermes" or "Hermes Trismegistus" (the "Thrice-great"),[11] tarot cards are therefore considered by some occultists (such as Tomberg) to be "Hermetic." However, even granting that tarot cards had an Egyptian origin, the images of the Tarot de Marseille are entirely Renaissance European: the clothing, the architecture, the furniture, the objects and the people—which include an emperor, an empress, a pope and a papess (female pope)—all did not exist during the ancient time of Hermes.

Even in such a "Europeanized" form, it's still rather bizarre that Tomberg would choose meditative images loosely derived from pre-Christian Egypt to use as Catholic "spiritual exercises"! For all the areas of concern that have been previously identified with the Ignatian *Spiritual Exercises* (in Chapter sub-section 4.3), at least most of the meditative imagery was safely taken from the Gospels.

Besides, there already exists within the Catholic Church a safe and effective developmental path leading to union with Christ-Jesus, and that is the sevenfold path of Mystic-Christianity. This tried and true developmental system has been successfully practiced within the various monastic orders for centuries, and exclusively employs meditative scenes from the life of Christ-Jesus—not from ancient Egypt or Renaissance Europe.

Rather than meditating on "The Magician, The Hanged Man, The Devil, The Lovers, The Chariot, The Moon, The Wheel of Fortune" and fifteen other non-biblical images, Mystic-Christianity focuses on the Gospel of John and seven profound events in the life of Christ-Jesus:

(1) the washing of the feet
(2) the scourging
(3) the crowning with thorns
(4) the crucifixion
(5) the mystic death
(6) the burial and resurrection
(7) the ascension

Why anyone—especially devout Catholics—would think that meditating on the images of the tarot is a superior method of Christian development, instead of that used in Mystic-Christianity, is certainly difficult to comprehend.

And what exactly is the goal, the end result of the

Tombergian tarot meditations? It certainly can't be mystical union with Christ-Jesus. If becoming Christ-like requires that the disciple follow in the footsteps of the Master, it's not likely that our Saviour would be leading us through the labyrinthine symbolic imagery[12] of a pseudo-Egyptian deck of cards so that we can finally reach him.

Therefore, one does not need to read very much of Tomberg's *Meditations on the Tarot* to conclude that the entire enterprise is a blind occult alleyway leading to spiritual darkness, rather than to the true light of Christ.

Even aside from the shadowy occultism and the unsavory appeal to magic contained in the *Meditations on the Tarot*, it's also astonishing how unabashedly arrogant and openly heretical Tomberg appears with certain of his written pronouncements. Once again on page 4, Tomberg wrote:

> The seven sacraments of the Church are the prismatic colours of the white light of one sole Mystery or Sacrament, known as the Second Birth, which the Master pointed out to Nicodemus in the nocturnal initiation conversation which He had with him. It is this which Christian Hermeticism understands by the *Great Initiation*.

For over two thousand years the Catholic Church has celebrated seven sacraments that are unquestioningly held to have been established by Christ-Jesus himself, and lovingly entrusted to his body the Church: (1) baptism, (2) confirmation, (3) Holy Communion (Eucharist), (4) holy matrimony (marriage), (5) holy orders, (6) penance (reconciliation), and (7) anointing of the sick. Tomberg here astoundingly claimed to have discovered an eighth, overarching sacrament—the sacrament of sacraments—which he termed the "sacrament of the second birth," which he also called the "Great Initiation"!

Other pronouncements that Tomberg made in *Meditations on the Tarot*, which attempt to combine his brand of tarot-occultism with Catholicism, are just plain silly. For example, commenting on "The Pope" meditation (or "Letter") on page 119, Tomberg wrote:

> The post of Pope or the Holy See is a formula of divine magic—just as the post of Emperor is—in the history of humanity. It is what is meant by the esoteric term *Petrus* (Peter) ... *Petrus* is the term in the Old and in the New Testament designating the divine, immovable ordinance or formula of divine magic.

I'm sure the present pope, Francis I, would be shocked and amused to learn that Tomberg and his present-day Catholic supporters regard him as the "grand magician" of the "Church of divine magic."

5.5 Tomberg's Legacy of Discord for Anthroposophy and for Catholicism

From what has been discussed thus far, it should be quite obvious that what Valentin Tomberg left behind "from beyond the grave" was not an amicable fusion of anthroposophy and Catholicism into a unified family of "Christian Hermeticism," but rather a trail of discord, distrust and animosity.

This was primarily due to the fact that Tomberg was not the high initiate that he fancied himself to be. As such, his esoteric enterprises did not have the sanction or the assistance of the rightful bodhisattva-masters of the West, Master John (Christian Rosenkreutz) and Master Zarathas (Master Jesus). Instead, as Tomberg readily admitted, he was "spiritually" inspired by shadowy French occultists and dark-magicians: Gérard Encausse (Papus; 1865–1916), Eliphas Lévi (1810–1875), Joséphin Péladan (1858–1918) and Stanislas de Guaita (1861–1897).

I also have well-known friends, but the greater part of them are in the spiritual world. All the more reason why I address them in these letters [meditations]. And how often in writing these lines did I feel the fraternal embrace of these friends, among them Papus, Guaita, Péladan, Eliphas Lévi ... (*Meditations on the Tarot*, 2002)

Any anthroposophist or any devout Catholic sincerely striving to harmoniously reconcile esoteric Christianity and exoteric Christianity will find no positive assistance from the life and written works of Valentin Tomberg.

CHAPTER 6

THE CHURCH OF ROME VERSUS THE
UNIVERSAL CHURCH

6.1 The Various Cultural Eras of Human Development

ACCORDING TO THE TEACHINGS of esoteric Christianity, the current phase of human development, what can loosely be termed the "Age of Western Civilization," began over 9,000 years ago (about a 1000 years after the last major Ice Age). Since the previous developmental phase is esoterically known as the "Atlantean Age," our current phase is also known as the "Post-Atlantean Age."

The Age of Western Civilization is expected to last over 15,000 years, and is comprised of seven smaller sub-phases of human development known as "cultural eras," each lasting 2,160 years. The first sub-phase, known as the "Ancient Indian" cultural era, began in 7227 BC, and lasted until 5067 BC. This sub-phase was succeeded by the "Ancient Persian" cultural era which lasted until 2907 BC. The well-known "Egypto-Chaldean" cultural era came next, and continued until 747 BC.

The "Graeco-Roman" cultural era, which gave birth to Christianity, lasted until 1423 AD. Esoterically, what is historically referred to as the "Renaissance" was not the "rebirth" of Graeco-Roman culture, but rather the end of the Graeco-Roman cultural era and the birth of the "Western European" cultural era (which includes the various European colonial offshoots around the world).[13] This is the cultural era in which we currently live, and which will continue until 3573 AD.

The Western European cultural era will be followed by two others: the "Slavic" cultural era (AD 3573–5733) and the "American" cultural era (AD 5733–7893).

Each of the seven cultural eras has been divinely destined to develop and further refine one particular vehicle (form) of human expression. The Ancient Indian cultural era was responsible for further developing the etheric body. The Ancient Persian cultural era was required to advance the astral body. In the time of the Egypto-Chaldean cultural era, the sentient soul was destined to be further developed (refer to Figures 2 and 3, if necessary).

During the Graeco-Roman cultural era, then, the intellectual soul was the focus of human development; in the same way that the consciousness soul is now the centre of vehicular development during the current Western European cultural era.

6.2 The Correspondence of Cultural Eras to Human Developmental Stages

The cultural eras that mankind in general undergoes throughout history quite naturally correspond to the seven-year developmental stages that each individual experiences in life. So, for example, the developmental stage from seven to fourteen, which subconsciously unfolds the etheric body, corresponds to the Ancient Indian cultural era. Likewise, the developmental stage from fourteen to twenty-one, during which the astral body is unfolded, corresponds to the Ancient Persian cultural era. From the ages of twenty-one to twenty-eight, individuals subconsciously unfold the sentient soul, which corresponds to the general development that occurred during the Egypto-Chaldean cultural era.

Between the ages of twenty-eight and thirty-five, the intellectual soul is subconsciously developed, which corresponds to the Graeco-Roman cultural era. The seven-year period from thirty-five to forty-two instinctively develops the consciousness soul, which corresponds to the general development that is to occur during the present cultural era, the Western European.

The Catholic Church, then, was instituted at a time when Graeco-Roman culture was the dominant civilizing force, and during which mankind in general was intended to develop the intellectual soul. This period of Catholic history corresponds to the developmental stage that takes place between twenty-eight and thirty-five for most individuals.

In accordance with the cultural impulses of the era, then, the nascent Christian Church incorporated strong elements of "Romanism" into its structure, organization and governance.

6.3   The Church of the Graeco-Roman Cultural Era

A superficial reading and casual grasp of Rudolf Steiner's numerous criticisms concerning the Catholicism of his day, can easily, but mistakenly, conclude that he regarded the Roman Catholic Church as obsolete, deleterious and destined for demise. Take, for example, a statement such as the following:

> The Roman Catholic Church, as a mighty corporation, represents the last withered remains of the civilization of

the fourth post-Atlantean epoch [the Graeco-Roman era]. It can be well authenticated in all detail that the Roman Catholic Church represents the last remnant of what was the right civilization for the fourth post-Atlantean epoch, what was justified right up to the middle of the Fifteenth Century, but what has now become a shadow. Of course products of a later evolution often herald their arrival in an earlier period, and its earlier products linger on into a later epoch, but in all essentials the Roman Catholic Church represents what was justifiable for Europe and its colonies up to the middle of the Fifteenth Century. (From a lecture given on 3 June 1920, entitled "Roman Catholicism")

From this particular quotation, we can readily see that Rudolf Steiner definitely regarded Medieval Roman Catholicism (not excusing the internal corruption or the moral failings of the priesthood during that time), as the correct and "justifiable" form of exoteric Christianity during the Graeco-Roman cultural era (747 BC–AD 1413).

Not surprisingly, since Christ-Jesus established his world-religion during the height of the Roman Empire, his nascent exoteric Church naturally incorporated integral features and elements of Roman culture and civilization. Especially when Nicene Christianity—as the official state religion—began to rapidly expand throughout the Roman Empire, Church leaders were quick to adopt effective Roman bureaucratic methods of organization and governance.

For example, in order to effectively govern a large empire, the Roman emperor Diocletian (245–311) divided the territory into one hundred provinces, that were each grouped into twelve larger units, called "dioceses." Each diocese was governed by an appointed official called a "vicarius." Similarly, in order to maintain and govern an expanding universal religion, the Catholic Church began to organized its various religious territories into numerous "dioceses," each governed by an officially appointed "vicar"; in this case, a local "bishop."

Furthermore, prior to Christianity, the pagan state religion of the Roman Republic was directed by the sacred college of pontiffs under the leadership of a high priest known as the "pontifex maximus" (the "great bridge-builder"). Moreover, the pontifex resided in Rome and was not simply a priest; he had political as well as religious authority, and could hold military command *and* magisterial office.

The pontifex (together with his advisory college) maintained universality and conformity of religious belief throughout the Roman Empire by administrating and enforcing the "jus divinum," or "divine law." The numerous religious traditions of the divine law were summarized and recorded in the form of authoritative principles, or "dogmas," and then bound together into a common "corpus," or text.

When the burgeoning Catholic Church became the state religion of the declining Roman Empire in 380 AD, church leaders soon adopted a similar hierarchical structure and leadership, with the pope assuming the position of pontifex maximus, and the college of cardinals assuming the role of the college of pontiffs. Even today, the pope still retains the title of "pontiff"; and similar to the Roman pontifex, the pope as high priest (or chief bishop) of the Catholic Church typically resides in Rome, and holds political as well as religious authority.

Similar to the Roman religious system as well, universality and conformity of Christian belief have been historically maintained and enforced by the collective establishment of religious dogma and canon law.

6.4   The Graeco-Roman Era and the Development of the Intellectual Soul

Since the Graeco-Roman cultural era was pre-destined to develop mankind's intellectual soul in a broad, general way, the period from 747 BC to AD 1413 can also be referred to as the "era of the Intellectual Soul." One of the principal characteristics of the intellectual soul (whether it is developed in a cultural era or as a developmental stage) is that knowledge begins to be acquired more consciously through intellectual (or abstract) concepts, rather than affectively understood through pictorial representations (that is, by visual symbols and imaginations).

Acquiring pictorial knowledge semi-consciously in an dreamlike, emotional way, is a salient feature of the sentient soul. This method of understanding was therefore a principal characteristic of the Egypto-Chaldean cultural era; otherwise known as the "era of the Sentient Soul." So when Christ-Jesus taught his general listeners through parables and allegorical stories, he was appealing to their sentient souls. To his more-advanced disciples, however, he could teach in clear, intellectual concepts directed at their intellectual souls. What can be accurately concluded from this Gospel information, then, is that the general public mentality of Christ's day still functioned at the level of the previous Egypto-Chaldean cultural era. Only a select few, during his day, were able to function at the intellectual soul level of the Graeco-Roman era in which they lived.

Regarding the intellectual soul, it is important to note that learning to consciously *receive* knowledge and understanding in the form of clear, intellectual concepts is a slow and gradual process. Moreover, learning to freely *generate* original knowledge in the form of clear, intellectual concepts is an even more advanced and difficult process, characteristic of the consciousness soul.

Consequently, only a few highly-advanced thinkers during the Graeco-Roman era were capable of generating original intellectual concepts and ideas—thinkers such as the philosophers Aristotle, Plato, St. Augustine and St. Thomas Aquinas. The best that the vast majority of mankind were cognitively capable of was the reception and incorporation of intellectual concepts on the basis of authority. In other words, during the Graeco-Roman era of the intellectual soul, it was appropriate and progressive in human development to accept concepts and ideas based on authority.

In the case of Catholic believers during the Graeco-Roman era, therefore, receiving knowledge and comprehension of Christian ideas on the basis of Church authority was not necessarily an unhealthy psychological activity. Rather the contrary. During the early centuries of the Church, agreement and uniformity of Christian belief was established by educated leaders through numerous, broadly-represented councils, and then gradually formalized into an extensive corpus of dogmas. These Catholic dogmas were (and still are) considered to be self-evident, infallible truths that faithful believers were obliged to unquestioningly accept.

For the typical, poorly-educated Christians throughout the Middle Ages, acquiring pre-established religious truth—on the authority of the Church and in the form of clear, intellectual dogmas—was a highly-effective and powerful cognitive assistance in developing the nascent intellectual soul.[14]

6.5 The Transition to the Western European Cultural Era and the Development of the Consciousness Soul

The transition from one cultural era to another is always a slow and gradual process. Furthermore, as with any profound change, the process is often fraught with discord, conflict and strife. Extreme reactionary proponents will often fight "tooth and nail" to resist necessary change, and to protectively perpetuate and preserve "the old ways." Likewise, extreme revolutionary proponents who are discontent with the slow pace of change, will often attempt to violently overthrow "the old order."

Due to the gradual nature of transitions between cultural eras, the impulses from a previous era will "overlap" into the succeeding one. Cultural impulses from a previous era will usually continue into the new one for several hundred years or more. Such was certainly the case with the transition from the Graeco-Roman era to the Western European era that began in AD 1413. Even to this day, 600 years later, the developmental impulses of the intellectual soul are still active in most cultural societies.

In fact, according to the observations of anthroposophical spiritual science, the vast majority of humanity today is still cognitively functioning at the level of the sentient soul—the level that characterized the Egypto-Chaldean era which existed 5000 years ago! As Rudolf Steiner stated in a lecture given on 3 November 1918, entitled "The Relation Between the Deeper European Impulses and Those of the Present Day":

> Today mankind as a whole is at the 'age' of the Sentient Soul, that is, between the ages of twenty-eight and twenty-one. This applies to the whole of mankind.

The shocking reality, then, is that the vast majority of human beings on earth today still acquire their knowledge and understanding in a dream-like, semi-conscious, emotional way through pictorial imagery, rather than through intellectual conceptualization. This certainly explains the powerful impact that visual media—television, cinema, computers and cell phones—have in mesmerizing and manipulating modern consciousness.

The current Western European cultural era is pre-destined to develop the consciousness soul. For the next 1558 years, more and more human beings will begin to consciously experience the reality of their own immortal souls. Moreover, they will also come to realize that true thinking is a superphysical activity of the soul. This realization will "spiritualize" intellectual thought, and enable thinkers to more freely generate their own life-imbued concepts from out of the superphysical world.

While developing the consciousness soul is the focus of our present cultural age, it is painfully obvious how far humanity, in general, is from this evolutionary goal. Since Rudolf Steiner established anthroposophy to assist in developing the consciousness soul, given the rudimentary level of "modern" human cognition, it is not in any way surprising that he met with widespread and fierce opposition and resistance.

6.6 The Cultural Inertia of the Nineteenth-Century Catholic Church

Given the fact that when Rudolf Steiner founded anthroposophy at the end of the nineteenth and beginning of the twentieth century, very few thinkers were advanced enough to develop the free and supersensible thinking that is characteristic of the consciousness soul, it was entirely predictable that conservative leaders within the Church would oppose his new cultural and spiritual initiative.

In somewhat of an ironic way, since the great throng of humanity was still cognitively functioning well below the level of the consciousness soul, the residual impulses of the Graeco-Roman era that were retained within the nineteenth-century Church, continued to be relevant and beneficial for a great many believers. Steiner certainly recognized this fact when he stated the following in a lecture given on 13 October 1911:

For those who desired to come to Christ, the Holy Communion was a complete equivalent of the esoteric path, if they could not take that path, and thus in the Holy Communion [of the Roman Catholic Church] they could find a real union with Christ. For all things have their time. Certainly, just as it is true in regard to the spiritual life that a quite new age is dawning, so is it true that the way to Christ which for centuries was the right one for many people will remain for centuries more the right one for many. Things pass over gradually into one another, and what was formerly right will gradually pass over into something else when people are ready for it. (Published in *From Jesus to Christ*, 1973)

It would also be fair to say, then, that Rudolf Steiner was not critical of Catholic Church dogma or conveying religious truth based on authority—per se. What he strongly objected to was the use of Church dogma and authority by ultra-conservative, militant Jesuits who were fiercely opposed to the new impulses of the consciousness soul; and who intended to stamp out those impulses by destroying Steiner together with anthroposophy.

If the conservative forces within the nineteenth-century Church were simply content to quietly ignore or peaceably tolerate the existence of anthroposophy, then there wouldn't have been such a fierce struggle on both sides. Since the establishment of anthroposophy was a super-earthly directive from St. Michael, the time-spirit responsible for the entire consciousness soul era, Rudolf Steiner could not allow himself or anthroposophy to be destroyed.

6.7 The Gradual Demise of "Romanism" Within the Catholic Church

When Rudolf Steiner spoke of the future demise of the

Roman Catholic Church, he was of course making this prediction based on the stifling, regressive forces that were predominant in the Church during the late-nineteenth and early-twentieth centuries. If in the future, the Church was unable to shake off these internal mummifying forces and to slowly begin incorporating the impulses of the consciousness soul, then human progress would surely leave the Church behind.

Collectively, these stagnant, reactionary forces can be termed, "Romanism." Romanism kept the Church anachronistically anchored geographically, administratively, liturgically and theologically to the centre of Rome and to ancient Roman culture. Rather than being the "universal" Church that Christ-Jesus had intended ("catholic" is Greek for "universal"), the Church of St. Peter had become increasingly sectarian and elitist.

For example, the liturgical celebration of the Mass (no matter where in the world) was exclusively conducted in Latin (the obsolete language of ancient Rome). Church decision-making was entirely centralized in Rome, and the Vatican administration (the Roman Curia), for centuries, was completely dominated and controlled by Italians. Even the pope and the College of Cardinals were almost always Italians. Theologically, this "Romanist" exclusivity was entrenched in the doctrinal assertion that "there was no salvation outside the Church"; that is, outside the Church of Rome.

Thankfully today, the Church of St. Peter has begun to shrug off the yoke of "Romanism" and to increasingly display true universality—true "catholicism." This tendency is clearly evident in Church literature and publications which often drop the word, "Roman," from their Catholic titles, such as the *Catechism of the Catholic Church*.

While Latin is still the official language of the Church, most parishes in the world today celebrate Mass in the "vernacular"; that is, in the native language of the country. Furthermore, even though the structure and the wording of Mass is standardized world-wide, Mass celebrations are free to incorporate local cultural elements regarding liturgical furnishings, architecture, vestments, music and artwork.

Significantly, the last three popes have not been Italian: Pope John Paul II was Polish, Pope Benedict XVI was German, and Pope Francis I is Argentinean. Not surprisingly, then, since cardinals can only be appointed by the pope, the three non-Italian popes have all appointed many non-Italian cardinals to the College. In the early 1900s, about 60% of the College of Cardinals were Italians. Today (2015), only about 20% are Italians.

Regarding the Italian stranglehold on the Roman Curia, the present pope, Francis I, has made it a priority to fundamentally reform this power-hungry bureaucratic body. In a scathing speech to the Curia given on 22 December 2014, Pope Francis stated:

> [T]he Curia—like the Church—cannot live without a vital, personal, authentic and solid relationship with Christ. A member of the Curia who is not daily nourished by that Food will become a bureaucrat (a formalist, a functionalist, a mere employee): a branch which withers, slowly dies and is then cast off ...
>
> The Curia is called constantly to improve and to grow in *communion, holiness and wisdom,* in order to carry out fully its mission. And yet, like any body, like any human body, it is also exposed to diseases, malfunctioning, infirmity. Here I would like to mention some of these probable diseases, "curial diseases." They are the more common diseases in our life in the Curia. They are diseases and temptations which weaken our service to the Lord.

Perhaps the best demonstration of the gradual precedence of Catholic universality over Roman sectarianism is the

Church's current understanding of the traditionally-held belief: "Outside the Church, there is no salvation." No longer is the word "Church" narrowly and exclusively interpreted to mean the "Church of Rome." "Church" is now inclusively understood to mean the entire body of Christian believers (including Catholic, Protestant and Orthodox), as well as other sincere seekers of God (such as Jewish, Muslim, Buddhist and non-denominational). As expressed in Section 847 of the *Catechism of the Catholic Church*:

> Those who, through no fault of their own, do not know the Gospel of Christ or his Church, but who nevertheless seek God with a sincere heart, and, moved by grace, try in their actions to do his will as they know it through the dictates of their conscience—those too may achieve eternal salvation.

CHAPTER 7

BETTER UNDERSTANDING CHURCH DOGMA

7.1 A Brief History of Church Dogma

OUTSIDE THE Catholic and Orthodox Churches, the words "dogma" and "dogmatism" are rarely used in a positive way these days. Almost always they are used as pejoratives; that is, as derogatory, disparaging terms. Both are commonly understood to refer to arrogant and narrow-minded ideas and opinions that are stubbornly held, often without positive proof or supportive evidence. Since "dogma" and "dogmatism," as originally understood and used by the ancient Greeks, did not have such scornful connotations, how did these once-benign terms later develop such a harsh, condemnatory reputation?

When the ancient Greeks first coined the word, "dogma," it was used in two distinct but similar ways. In the one instance it was used philosophically to apply to self-evident or "a priori" truths, such as "a square has four sides" or "if God exists, then he must be infinite and eternal." In the second instance, dogma was used politically to refer to a public edict, decree or proclamation made by a civil authority. A biblical example of this particular usage during later Roman times is recorded in Luke 2:1: "And it came to pass, that in those days there went out a decree [dogma] from Caesar Augustus."

The similarity in these two distinct usages is that in both cases, critical argumentation and dispute were regarded as futile, unproductive and unnecessary. As such, one was expected to give unquestioning assent to the proclaimed dogma.

When dogma first began to be used by the early Christian Church, a unique and significant fusion was possible after 380 when Emperor Theodosius I proclaimed Christianity to be the state religion of the Roman Empire. With the Edict of Milan, the struggling Christian Church acquired universal ("catholic") ecclesiastical authority, as well as influential and forceful political authority.

Any self-evident theological truth proclaimed by the Church of Rome, therefore, also carried the commanding weight of a political or state decree. Any dogma established by the Church of Rome henceforth was regarded as both a self-evident theological truth *and* a state edict of the Roman Empire. Needless to say, this resulted in enormous pressure for all Roman citizens to accept Church dogma without serious question or open dissent.

As a result, the obstinate doubt or rejection of Church dogma—what was defined as "heresy"—carried a double consequence: ecclesiastical censure by the Church, and civil condemnation by the Roman state. While heretics were consequently treated rather harshly by overzealous and intolerant Church and state authorities, for the vast number of uneducated, medieval Roman citizens, the unquestioning acceptance of Church dogma had an enormously positive influence instead.

7.2   The Purpose of Church Dogma and How it is Established

Basically understood, the various dogmas of the Church are enduring principles of faith and morals that promote saintliness and holiness in order to achieve eternal salvation in heaven. As such, they are intended to assist the Christian believer to follow in the footsteps of Christ-Jesus; and thereby become an adopted "son" or "daughter" of God. The recognized sources of Church dogma have been the biblical teachings of Christ-Jesus, the biblical teachings of the apostles and evangelists, widespread and enduring Church tradition, and the "magisterial" pronouncements[15] of the Church.

Contrary to popular misconception, the pope does not determine Church dogma unilaterally; that is, entirely on his own authority, and without the universal agreement of the world-bishops. Though the official pronouncement of a particular dogma (such as the Immaculate Conception of Mary by Pope Pius IX in 1854, and the Assumption of Mary by Pope Pius XII in 1950) may be done "ex cathedra"; that is, by papal authority, the decision to do so was previously made in communion with the world-bishops.

Since Church dogmas are regarded as self-evident truths that remain valid, unchanged, inerrant and enduring throughout time, they are also termed, "infallible truths" or "infallibly declared" dogmas. Though there is no official Catholic compilation of Church dogma, Dr. Ludwig Ott (1906–1985) in *Fundamentals of Church Dogma* (2009) has provided a comprehensive listing of 426 infallible truths. A few examples that Ott has identified are:

1.   There is only one God
2.   God is eternal
3.   The Trinity of God can only be known through divine revelation

4. Every human being possesses an individual soul
5. The divine and the human natures are united hypostatically in Christ; that is, joined to each other in one person
6. The Son of God became man in order to redeem men
7. Mary was conceived without stain of original sin
8. The Church was founded by the God-Man, Jesus Christ
9. The body and the blood of Christ together with his soul and his divinity, and therefore the whole Christ, are truly present in the Eucharist
10. All human beings subject to original sin are subject to the law of death

Aside from a handful of Church theologians and clergy, few ordinary Catholics are familiar with the totality of declared dogma. The extent of most Catholic belief is contained within the Nicene Creed[16] or the Apostles' Creed[17] which are professed by the faithful at every Mass.

7.3 Not All Catholic Teaching is Infallible Dogma

A great many Catholics and non-Catholics alike are entirely unaware that there are four levels of teaching (that is, truth) within the Church of St. Peter. The first level, of course, are the divinely-revealed, *infallible teachings* of the Church. The Catholic faithful are expected to willingly assent to these teachings. Moreover, these dogmatic truths are not open to debate or dispute. To do so is regarded as "heresy"; and since the dissenter is considered to be "out of communion" with the Church, he or she may not receive the sacrament of Holy Communion.

The second level of doctrine is comprised of the non-revealed, *definitive teachings* of the Church. Those these teachings have not been infallibly declared, the Catholic faithful are still obligated to willingly assent to them. Reluctance to do so is not considered to be heresy, but one is considered to be "in serious error," and thereby excluded from receiving Holy Communion. Some examples of definitive teachings that are not open to debate or dispute are the exclusive ordination of men, and the illicitness of abortion and euthanasia.

The third level of doctrine is comprised of the *authoritative teachings* of the Church. Though these teachings are also not infallible (and therefore not dogmas), the faithful are expected to assent to them with "religious submission of will and intellect," and thereby grant the Church the presumption of truthfulness and good judgement. Some examples of authoritative teaching are the Church's definition of marriage and the Church's position on capital punishment. Non-obedience is regarded as "dissent." There must be a very compelling reason to disagree with these teachings or, once again, the dissident is not in communion with the Church.

The fourth level of doctrine is comprised of the *authentic teachings* of the Church. These teachings are usually established by the bishops, either individually or in various councils, to which the faithful must grant a "religious assent of soul." If there is disagreement, it must be for good cause and it must be respectful. One local example is the practice of bowing before receiving communion. Non-compliance is regarded as "disobedience."

7.4 The Freedom of Conscience and Religion

Even though to be a "member in good faith" each and every Catholic is expected to willingly assent to and abide by the infallible dogmas of the Church, today's Code of Canon Law recognizes that: "No one is ever permitted to coerce persons to embrace the Catholic faith against their conscience." Moreover, the Declaration on Religious Freedom, entitled "Dignitatis Humanae," that was issued by Paul VI on 7 December 1965 has further stated:

> In all his activity a man is bound to follow his conscience in order that he may come to God, the end and purpose of life. It follows that he is not to be forced to act in a manner contrary to his conscience. Nor, on the other hand, is he to be restrained from acting in accordance with his conscience, especially in matters religious. The reason is that the exercise of religion, of its very nature, consists before all else in those internal, voluntary and free acts whereby man sets the course of his life directly toward God. No merely human power can either command or prohibit acts of this kind.

Regarding religious freedom, Paul VI has also stated in the same Declaration:

> This Vatican Council declares that the human person has a right to religious freedom. This freedom means that all men are to be immune from coercion on the part of individuals or of social groups and of any human power, in such wise that no one is to be forced to act in a manner contrary to his own beliefs, whether privately or publicly, whether alone or in association with others, within due limits.

From critical comments made by Rudolf Steiner in a lecture given on 30 May 1920 entitled "Roman Catholicism," it would appear that the Church in his day did not support freedom of conscience or religion. Steiner notes that in the papal encyclical of Pius IX, entitled "Quanta Cura" (1864), it is stated that Gregory XVI regarded the belief that "liberty of conscience and worship is each man's personal right" to be an "insanity."

However, by placing this quotation in the context of the

entire encyclical, it is best understood that Pius IX regarded freedom of conscience and religion to be "God-given" rights. He rejected the atheistic notion that these freedoms are simply "personal" or "secular" rights that can be subjectively applied. It is also clear from the rest of the encyclical that Pius IX was theologically opposed to "freedom of conscience and religion" being used by atheistic thinkers as rationalistic excuses to promote an anti-religious, secular model of society.

Nevertheless, it is also important to acknowledge that in centuries past, these fundamental principles of conscience and religious freedom were not always respected or properly applied by powerful officials within the Catholic Church. The Spanish Inquisition and the Albigensian Crusade are two well-known historical examples of cruel and violent enforcement of dogmatic Church doctrine. The use of torture and execution as a means of converting others to Christianity was and is, of course, completely contrary to the compassionate, non-violent teachings of Christ-Jesus. His true Church would never engage in such despicable practices; but rather, it was always evil-minded and corrupt officials within the Church who were intent on destroying Christ's institution of freedom and love, and subverting it into a false church of coercion and hate.

While one is certainly free these days to either accept or reject the infallible dogmas of the Catholic Church, it would logically be rather difficult to be simultaneously a faithful practitioner, as well as a confirmed heretic. By rejecting the foundational beliefs upon which the Church is erected, the entire edifice is weakened and left without strong theological support.

7.5 Are Dogmas a Hindrance to Modern Thinking?

There is a popular notion in today's world that dogma,

particularly Church dogma, is a thing of the past that has no place in our modern, free-thinking intellectual atmosphere.[18] In actual fact, however, this idea is naïve, superficial, arrogant and entirely incorrect. The reality is that every modern ideological discipline, such as mathematics, science, philosophy, medicine, music and art (as well as religion) is supported and enabled by required axiomatic premises and fundamental presuppositions—that is, dogmas. Without these dogmatic antecedents, each of these disciplines could not exist.

Take mathematics, for example. Without accepting and abiding by the axiomatic rules of addition, subtraction, multiplication and division: such as "1 + 1 = 2" and "you cannot divide by 0"—the practice of mathematics is impossible. Likewise, philosophy is impossible to pursue without assenting to the axiomatic rules of logic, such as the "law of identity" (A is A), and the "law of non-contradiction" (A is not non-A). Even the entire edifice of modern science is utterly dependent on a number of philosophical axioms, such as:

1. The world and nature are real
2. Nature and the real world are knowable and comprehensible by the human mind
3. There are laws that govern the universe and everything in it
4. Those laws are knowable and comprehensible

Rather than hindering the ability to generate free thought, the self-evident axioms (dogmas) that underlie the variety of modern ideological pursuits actual provide the necessary foundation for thought. The theological dogmas of the Catholic Church are no exception, and likewise are intended to assist the faithful in understanding the world that surrounds them (that is, God and his creation).

In a lecture given on 4 April 1906, entitled "The Children

of Lucifer," Rudolf Steiner also acknowledged the positive use of dogma, including Church dogma:

> The dogma of the Church can certainly contain truth. In this sense a Pythagorean axiom can be a dogma for those who understand it. But when they understand it, it becomes bright, clear knowledge for them. Dogmas are presented as founded on authority. When we understand them, they become clear knowledge.

7.6 The Misuse of Church Dogma

While dogmas can certainly express valuable, self-evident truth, and thereby enable and promote freedom of thought, they can also be used by unscrupulous individuals to control and suppress the generation of free thought.

As has been discussed previously, particularly in Chapter 4, during the late-nineteenth century there were powerful and influential renegade clergymen (mostly Jesuit) who were covertly promoting a distorted future-vision of the universal Church. Their totalitarian intention was to establish complete world-wide dominance and control of *all* religion (not just Christian) by the Vatican Curia of Rome.

In order to accomplish this global, dictatorial monopoly of religion, these rogue Jesuits entered into a secret, unholy alliance with equally vainglorious Masonic associations that were intent on establishing totalitarian control of the global economy and global politics—what they referred to as the "New World Order." Complete autocratic control of religious belief would be accomplished by the strict enforcement of religious dogma that was "infallibly" determined by the pope and the Roman Curia.

As preparatory steps in establishing despotic Vatican control of religious belief, the "Dogma of Papal Infallibility" was declared in 1870, and the "Oath Against Modernism" was imposed in 1910. Fortunately over time, these two conservative initiatives did little to stifle the generation of positive religious thought, both inside and outside the Church. Moreover, though certain secret brotherhoods (particularly in the West) are still striving to establish their New World Order, proponents of dogmatic authoritarianism within the modern Catholic Church have little power and influence, and are largely silenced.

7.7 The Dogma of Papal Infallibility

Without a doubt, the dogma that is best known by non-Catholics, and also the one that is least understood is the "dogma of papal infallibility." The prevalent and widespread misunderstanding is that Catholics believe that the pope (whoever it may be) is infallible in all that he does; that is, the pope never makes a mistake or commits an error of any kind in his daily actions or speech. Predictably, those who hold to such a misconception are alarmed by and critical of such a preposterous dogma.

The truth of the matter is, however, that this dogma only applies to the pope when he is making an official declaration as the supreme head of the Catholic Church (that is, "ex cathedra") on a belief of faith or morals, that is to be universally affirmed by the entire Church. In essence, the dogma states that when the pope, on behalf of Christ-Jesus, declares a God-given belief to be true, he doesn't make a mistake in doing so. It is only in this very rare and special circumstance that the pope is considered "infallible." In all other areas of his life, the pope is regarded as just as "fallible" as the rest of humanity.

Even though the idea of papal infallibility has been espoused and exercised by the Church for hundreds of years, it was not until 1870 that it was officially declared as an "infallible truth" by the First Vatican Council of 1869–1870. Since then, papal infallibility has been sparingly exercised only once—the dogma concerning the "Assumption of Mary" by Pius XII in 1950. Obviously, most popes have been exceedingly cautious and reluctant to make an "infallible" declaration. Pope John XXIII (1881–1963), for example, once admitted: "I am only infallible if I speak infallibly; but I shall never do that, so I am not infallible." More recently, Pope Benedict XVI (b.1927) similarly stated: "The Pope is not an oracle; he is infallible in very rare situations, as we know."

Though in principle the pope can unilaterally exercise papal infallibility, it is highly unlikely that this will ever occur. Since an infallible declaration must be accepted by the entire Church, it would obviously require the full consent of the Council of Bishops beforehand.

In summary, then, though there may have been nefarious intentions by fanatics within the late-nineteenth century Church to use the dogma of papal infallibility (and the Oath Against Modernism) to autocratically control worldwide religious belief, fortunately this has failed to occur.

7.8 The Oath Against Modernism

In the lecture given on 3 June 1920 entitled "Roman Catholicism," Rudolf Steiner accurately observed that since 1850 a "rising tide of Darwinism … [and] naturalism" had begun to sweep over the civilized world in general and European society in particular. Also during that time, Steiner indicated that the following Marxist attitude (as expressed by Frederick Engels: 1820–1895) was becoming increasingly popular "among the widest circles of the European population":

Religion, which represents a fantastic reflex in the minds

of human beings concerning their relations to one another and to nature, is doomed to natural decay through the victorious growth of the scientific, clear and naturalistic grasp of reality, which is bound to develop parallel with the establishment of a planned society

Concerning the rising tide of atheistic, materialistic ideology that began in the late-nineteenth century, Steiner himself observed that:

The so-called 'enlightened' humanity of today is still soundly asleep to the fact that such a view is coming. But the Roman Catholic Church is awake; she alone in fact is awake and working systematically against the approaching storm. She works against it in her own way.

This philosophical tsunami that swept over somnolent humanity was termed, "modernism." Modernism grew out of the post-Renaissance, philosophical soil of "humanism"[19] and "rationalism";[20] and was broadly characterized by a blanket rejection of past cultural tradition, particularly religious belief. By denouncing the heritage of the past as obsolete, modernism attempted to re-create and re-establish—to "modernized"—art, literature, music, architecture, philosophy, politics, economics, technology and science. By rejecting religious and spiritual tradition and belief, modernism spawned a host of interconnected atheistic ideologies and movements, such as "Darwinism,"[21] "naturalism,"[22] "materialism,"[23] "relativism,"[24] "communism,"[25] "futurism,"[26] "scientism"[27] and "secularism."[28] Because of this, Pius X considered modernism to be "the synthesis of all heresies."

While Steiner acknowledged that the Catholic Church of his day was fully aware of the rapid increase and future impact of nineteenth-century modernism, he contends that the Church's reaction was entirely contrary to that of a free and open religious institution—due primarily to the ultra-conservative, absolutist influence of fundamentalist Jesuits. The result was a weakening of the "universal, Catholic" element of the Church, and a strengthening of the "sectarian, Roman" element of the Church.

In other words, in order to meet the sweeping onrush of modernist ideology, the nineteenth-century Church decided to "circle the wagons"; that is, to further centralize Vatican power and authority in Rome, and to additionally increase the strict, unquestioning, worldwide enforcement of Church dogma. To this end, Pius X in 1910 imposed the "Oath Against Modernism" on "all clergy, pastors, confessors, preachers, religious superiors, and professors in philosophical-theological seminaries."

Even though the oath itself is a marvelous summary of modernist ideology and a succinct distillation of Catholic doctrine, it was the authoritarian intent, rather than the actual content that had a stultifying effect on twentieth-century Catholic thought and practice. The liberating influences of the Second Vatican Council (1962–1965), eventually rescinded the oath in 1967. Presently, no one within the Church is compelled to take the oath, though it is still taken voluntarily by some members.

7.9   The Positive Role of Authority and Obedience

In our current age of supposedly free and unfettered thinking, "authority" and "obedience" are popularly regarded as unwanted and unnecessary intellectual restrictions. This simplistic generalization does not always apply. In many familiar instances, reliance on authority and willing obedience instead enable and facilitate freedom of thought and expression.

While "thinking for oneself" is certainly extolled and encouraged in today's world, the overwhelming volume and rapidity of new factual material, new scientific discovery, new technological innovation and new media communication makes it extremely difficult for the ordinary thinker to personally test and validate the constant deluge of new information. As a result, the ordinary thinker finds it increasingly necessary to rely on government agencies, certification boards, scientific tribunals, peer review counsels, standards committees or panels of experts—that is, external authority—in order to determine the truth or falsehood of all this information.

Few of us, for instance, have bothered to personally validate any new cosmological discovery (say, the existence of "dark matter"); or to test any new therapeutic drug (say, medical marijuana); or to determine the safety of any new technology (say, cell-phone radiation); or to assess the health benefits of any new food product (say, genetically-modified wheat). The disturbing reality is, in today's free-thinking age, we are crucially dependent on a host of external authorities for our day-to-day existence and well-being. As long as these various authorities are honest and trustworthy, they are of immense benefit, and contribute positively to a free and healthy thought-life.

Therefore, it is entirely hypocritical for those who subscribe to the scientific worldview to denigrate and condemn the existence and activity of a body of religious authority, such as the magisterium of the Catholic Church. In the same way that a peer review committee (as a jury of scientific experts) assesses and determines the validity or truthfulness of scientific ideas, so does the magisterium of the Church (as a jury of religious experts) assess and determines the validity or truthfulness of religious ideas. In both cases, as long as the authorities are honest and trustworthy, they are of benefit in determining truth or falsehood. Moreover, a healthy reliance on truthful authority does not dissuade us from continuing to develop our own innate sense of the truth, and to exercise our own reliable judgement.

It could even be argued that in today's pervasive scientific worldview, more people place an unquestioning blind faith in scientific authority, than the genuine faith that occurs with religious belief.

Once we become convinced of a particular truth by own reasonable investigation or by accepting the judgement of a reliable authority, it only makes sense to embrace and abide by that truth. Obedience to the truth connects us with reality, while disobedience to the truth dissociates us from the world. If God does exist, for example, and the entire world is his creation (and this is a self-evident truth or dogma), then denying this truth will obviously disconnect us from the real world.

Moreover, obedience to the truth does not restrict our freedom; but rather, it enables us to be free. Obeying the law of gravity (a natural truth), for example, enables us to overcome it and to experience the freedom of flight. Ignoring the truth of gravity will only keep us fettered to the earth. This connection of truth and freedom was biblically emphasized by Christ-Jesus in John 8:32: "[Y]ou will know the truth, and the truth will make you free."

7.10 The Positive Roles of Catholicism and Anthroposophy in the Modern World

While Rudolf Steiner readily acknowledged that the late-nineteenth century Catholic Church was fully "awake" to the approaching "storm" of modernist ideology, he was nevertheless highly critical of the Church's overprotective response to this storm. In other words, Steiner fully agreed with the Church that the secular, materialistic and atheistic impulses of modernist ideology would have catastrophic consequences for future society in general and religion in particular. Steiner's criticism was only in regard to the Church's reaction to the approaching modernist upheaval. Rather than compassionately reaching out to a world in turmoil and providing a convincing, comforting, free-to-accept spiritual alternative, Steiner felt that the Church fell prey to Jesuit fundamentalism and instead became more insular, defensive and dogmatically authoritarian. In short, rather than overcoming the harmful social ideology of modernism with peaceful truth and understanding, the Church authorities decided to wage doctrinal war instead.

Since Steiner also understood the devastating potential of modernist ideology, as an initiate-representative of esoteric Christianity, he also took important steps to dispel the looming storm. In order to counteract the atheistic, anti-religious worldview of materialistic science, Rudolf Steiner established an opposing science—a "science of the spirit"—anthroposophy. Anthroposophy, then, began as a resistance movement (and society) to materialistic modernism.

In the case of anthroposophy, it purposely avoided erecting protective walls of dogmatic truth as a barrier against modernist ideas (as did the Catholic Church). Instead, anthroposophy as a spiritual science, deliberately employed the scientific method against materialistic science. By doing so, Steiner was able to freely ascertain and study the supernatural, spiritual world without recourse to divine revelation or pre-established dogma. In Steiner's view, spiritual science was the best way of confronting and counteracting the harmful effects of modernism.

Even so, Steiner never denied that the nineteenth-century Catholic Church had the inherent freedom to react differently towards modernism; and that if it had, the Church could have been more of a positive social force during his time.[29] In fact, the Catholic Church in the twenty-first century is clearly endeavoring to compassionately reach out to a secular, "Godless" world that is mired in a "culture of death" where human life has little value. In many instances today, the Catholic Church is the only universal institution that actively defends and promotes the God-given dignity of every human life from conception until its natural end.

By remaining true to its ageless spiritual values and not succumbing to the pressures of ephemeral social change, the Church for many has been a comforting bulwark in the storm of modern materialism. Since the Church *is* the faithful repository of great spiritual truth, it isn't necessary to force that truth on others. Those that are spiritually lost, spiritually deprived and spiritually hungry will naturally seek out a beacon of true spiritual light, especially when that light is made freely available without coercion.

When it comes to opposing modernism, then, the Catholic Church and anthroposophy have the same goal: to preserve and promote human access to the spiritual world. Of course each must do this in different ways. As an institution of exoteric Christianity, the Catholic Church does this best by faithfully guarding and sharing the God-given truths that have been revealed through Christ-Jesus, the apostles, the evangelists and the magisterium. While the sharing and conveyance of these eternal truths may require adaptation and change from age to age, the essence of these eternal truths remains unaltered. The discovery of additional truth from non-religious sources (such as science and philosophy) can certainly be incorporated from time to time when they don't contradict the eternal truths that are already held.

As an institution of esoteric Christianity, anthroposophy is expected to not simply preserve truth from the past, but to continually strive for higher and deeper truth, and to change and adapt its methods of investigation to suit the demands of each particular age. In past centuries, esoteric Christianity took the form of a secret brotherhood (the Knights of the

Holy Grail), and later a hidden fraternity (the Order of the Rose Cross). At the present time, it takes the form of a public society that promotes spiritual science (the General Anthroposophical Society). In the future, esoteric Christianity is expected to once again assume a different external form that is more in tune with a new age.

CHAPTER 8

ANTHROPOSOPHICAL CHRISTOLOGY AND THE DOCTRINE OF REPEATED LIVES

8.1 Anthroposophical Support of Catholic Dogma

IT MAY COME as a bit of a shock and surprise for anthroposophical critics and Catholic critics alike to discover that even though Rudolf Steiner was staunchly critical of the authoritarian imposition of Church dogmas in the modern age of intellectual freedom, he was rarely critical of the spiritual content of the dogmas themselves. In fact, his own independent spiritual scientific investigations very often confirmed and validated the truths of Catholic dogma.

Steiner also felt that much of the sublime spiritual wisdom and truth contained in Catholic dogma had become increasingly rigidified and deadened over the centuries. Moreover, he bemoaned the fact that the once-uplifting religious truth that was faithfully guarded by the Catholic Church was no longer appreciated or understood, particularly in the protestant denominations. In a lecture given on 24 April 1921, entitled "Materialism and the Task of

Anthroposophy," Steiner stated the following:

> Now, if we wish to comprehend our modern age, we
> must not forget what these Roman-Catholic dogmas
> couched in Roman political concepts are fundamentally
> all about. Among them are doctrines of great significance,
> splendid doctrines. There is, above all, the doctrine of the
> Trinity, which, in other terminology of later times, points
> to the Father, the Son, and the Spirit. An ancient and
> profound primordial wisdom was frozen into this
> doctrine, something great and mighty that human
> perception once possessed instinctively. Yet, only the
> brilliant, inspired insight of a few could fathom what is
> contained in such a doctrine ...

There were dogmas concerning the birth, the nature of
Christ Jesus, the death, the Resurrection, and the
Ascension. Finally, there were dogmas establishing the
various festivals; and all this was basically the skeleton,
the silhouette of a wondrous, ancient wisdom ... The
content of what was thus expressed in dogmas, in the
most sublime dogmas, such as the dogma of the
transubstantiation of the bread and wine into the body
and blood of Christ, could spread because it was clothed
in the form of an ancient, sacred cult, namely, the
Sacrifice of the Mass ... Those aspects lived on that you
know as the sacraments. They were intended to lift the
human being out of the ordinary material life through the
agency of the Church, so to speak, into a higher, spiritual
sphere ...

> Because of its significant content and because
> people basically had nothing else with which to
> establish a relationship to the super-sensible worlds,
> all these doctrines together were something that
> affected minds striving for such higher knowledge.
> Due to the ritual and the simple narration of the

Gospel, however, these doctrines could also unfold that form of activity that gained influence over the broad masses of Europe's population ...

The Sacrifice of the Mass, a religious act of the greatest cosmic significance, turned into an external, symbolic act because it was no longer understood. The sacrament of the Transubstantiation, which had survived through the Middle Ages and which has profound cosmic significance, became part of purely intellectual disputes ...

[T]he ancient spirituality—the spirituality to which there is still a connection through dogmas—did once dwell in what has become a skeleton, a shadow. Among the more recent Protestant confessions, where a compromise is being tried out, such a connection is no longer alive.

8.2 The "Greater Mysteries" of Anthroposophy and the "Lesser Mysteries" of Catholicism

As a true science (albeit a spiritual one), anthroposophy is not to accept any particular fact or truth solely on the basis of authority. Even though a dogma of the Church may indeed be an infallible truth, anthroposophical spiritual science is still compelled to investigate, test and validate all dogmatic assertions. Since authentic science and genuine religion both seek the same ultimate truth,[30] it shouldn't be surprising that Steiner's anthroposophical investigations very often validated Catholic infallible truth.

In fact, as a modern-day expression of esoteric Christianity, anthroposophy's core mission was (and is) to deepen, expand and promulgate the "greater mysteries" of Christianity. As a Christian initiate, then, Rudolf Steiner's intent was never to denigrate, disparage or disprove the dogmatic truths of the Catholic Church; but rather to reawaken, revivify, restore and reactivate the profound spiritual truths that lay hidden or sleeping within them. Perceptive Catholics today are equally concerned that a great many members of the Church (laity *and* clergy) don't really understand or appreciate the "cosmic significance" of Catholic doctrine. While the "lesser mysteries" of Christianity may have temporarily withered under the scorching light of materialistic intellectualism, the fountain of anthroposophical knowledge can certainly help restore them to health and vitality.

Though the spiritual scientific information conveyed in anthroposophy may appear to be radically different than Catholic doctrine, most often it is only because the teachings of esoteric Christianity are far more detailed and complex, not contrary. Seen in this light, Catholic dogmas are basically concise and abbreviated truths that have been simplified for easier understanding.

Take for instance the religious doctrine of Adam and Eve. Even though the Catholic Church recognizes that the Genesis account of creation is allegorical and symbolic,[31] it is still a matter of dogmatic belief that all of humanity sprang from one ancestral pair (whatever their names). This of course has been an embarrassing intellectual stumbling block for Catholic theologians who wish to be taken seriously by the scientific community. Nevertheless, even natural science has recently postulated the existence of "Mitochondrial Eve," a prehistoric African woman who is the genetic mother of all DNA existing today.

Since the Church has very little to dogmatically declare concerning our original ancestral couple, it leaves further details open to scientific speculation and investigation. In the case of anthroposophical spiritual science, the independent research of Rudolf Steiner—though much more complex and detailed—reaffirms the existence of a primal, original couple. In a lecture given on 18 September 1909 on the topic of the Gospel of St. Luke, Steiner explained:

> During the Lemurian epoch there was actually a time when it may be said—with approximate accuracy at any rate—that there was a single couple in existence, *one main pair* (*Haupt-paar*) which had retained sufficient strength to master the stubborn substance and to incarnate on the Earth, to 'hold out' as it were through the period when the Moon was separating from the Earth. This separation made it possible again for human substance to be refined and rendered suitable to receive the weaker souls; the descendants of this one main pair were therefore able to live in more pliable substance than had been available before the separation of the Moon. Then, by degrees, all the souls returned to the Earth from Mars, Jupiter, Venus, Mercury and Saturn; and through propagation the souls gradually returning to the Earth from the planets constituted the descendants of the first main pair.
>
> Thus the Earth was re-peopled. And during the latter part of the Lemurian until far into the Atlantean epoch, an ever-increasing number of souls descended, having waited on the other planets until a time came when they were able to incarnate in earthly bodies. In this way the Earth was re-populated and the Atlantean peoples came into existence ...

No doubt, Catholic theologians unfamiliar with the basic research of spiritual science will find Steiner's quoted information overly complicated and difficult to understand. Nevertheless, this doesn't mean that this information is incorrect or heretical, but simply the comprehensive results of objective scientific investigation. And most importantly, the basic conclusion of this spiritual scientific research is in agreement with related Catholic dogma. When fully understood, then, the greater mysteries of esoteric Christianity will always support, supplement and enhance the lesser mysteries of exoteric Christianity.

8.3   Anthroposophy and the Dogmas of Mary: "Immaculate Conception," "Perpetual Virginity" and "Assumption"

While anthroposophical spiritual science is in full agreement with the more familiar self-evident truths of Catholic dogma—such as the existence and attributes of God; original sin and the fall from grace; the incarnation of Christ-Jesus and his role in salvation; and the spiritual value of the Church's sacraments—perhaps surprising to many is the fact that Steiner's independent research also confirmed and elaborated some of the lesser known dogmas of the Church. Three such examples pertain to Blessed Mary, the mother of Jesus: they are the dogmas of "Immaculate Conception," "Perpetual Virginity" and "Assumption."

As declared by Pius IX in 1854, the dogma of the Immaculate Conception states:

> The most Blessed Mary was, from the first moment of her conception, by a singular grace and privilege of almighty God and by virtue of the merits of Jesus Christ, Saviour of the human race, preserved immune from all stain of original sin. (Paragraph 491 of the *Catechism of the Catholic Church*)

As understood, reinforced and elaborated by anthroposophical spiritual science, the uniquely-special soul described in Luke's gospel as Mary, the mother of Jesus, had no prior incarnations on earth. Instead, during the Lemurian Age, higher spiritual beings safeguarded and protected this nascent soul from the perfidious Luciferic interference which resulted in humanity's "fall" from heavenly paradise into earthly materiality. In other words, when Luke's Mary incarnated for the first time, her soul was entirely free from the effects of primordial Luciferic interference; and therefore "immaculate" or untarnished by the stain of original sin.

Once again, though the detailed esoteric explanation obviously differs from that of familiar Catholic theology, the resultant conclusion is the same.

Similarly with the dogma of Mary's "Perpetual Virginity." As stated in Paragraph 499 of the *Catechism of the Catholic Church*:

> The deepening of faith in the virginal motherhood led the Church to confess Mary's real and perpetual virginity even in the act of giving birth to the Son of God made man. In fact, Christ's birth "did not diminish his mother's virginal integrity but sanctified it"; and so the liturgy of the Church celebrates Mary as Aeiparthenos, or the "Ever-virgin."

Though the esoteric details of Rudolf Steiner's spiritual scientific research significantly differ from the accepted theology of the Church, the conclusion is once again the same. In a lecture given on 3 July 1909 entitled "What Occurred at the Baptism?" Steiner stated:

> At the same moment in which the Spirit of Christ descended into the body of Jesus of Nazareth and the transformation occurred as described, an influence was exerted upon the Mother of Jesus of Nazareth as well. It consisted in her regaining her virginity at this moment of the Baptism; that is, her inner organism reverted to the state existing before puberty. At the birth of the Christ, the Mother of Jesus of Nazareth became a virgin.

Concerning the Catholic dogma of the "Assumption of Mary" that was infallibly declared (ex cathedra) by Pius XII in

1950, Paragraph 966 of the *Catechism of the Catholic Church* states:

> "Finally the Immaculate Virgin, preserved free from all stain of original sin, when the course of her earthly life was finished, was taken up body and soul into heavenly glory, and exalted by the Lord as Queen over all things, so that she might be the more fully conformed to her Son, the Lord of lords and conqueror of sin and death." The Assumption of the Blessed Virgin is a singular participation in her Son's Resurrection and an anticipation of the resurrection of other Christians.

Regarding this particular Church dogma, Rudolf Steiner did not provide much in the way of a detailed esoteric background; but simply to state:

> Only the Christ and Mary were able to take their bodies up into the fixed star heaven ...

> Jesus and Mary had hallowed their physical body to such a degree that they were able to take it with them to the highest regions. (From a lecture given on 11 February 1906 entitled, "The Medieval View of the World in Dante's Divine Comedy")

Even though many more examples could be provided, just by examining the three preceding Catholic dogmas it should be evident to Catholic and anthroposophical critics alike that the truths (or greater mysteries) of esoteric Christianity are meant to complement and enrich the dogmatic truths (or lesser mysteries) of exoteric Christianity. As long as there is an amicable independence maintained between these two separate streams of Christian mystery-truth, there should be no mutual fear, hostility or suspicion that each side is secretly plotting the demise of the other.

8.4 Reconciling Anthroposophical Christology[32] with Catholic Theology

One particular area where anthroposophical investigation appears to dramatically differ from familiar Catholic theology concerns the person of Christ-Jesus. Even though the concluding truths of spiritual science once again harmonize with Church dogma, unfortunately it is easy to get distracted by the wealth of Steiner's original clairvoyant discoveries, and thereby reach incorrect conclusions. This is just as easy for anthroposophical students as it is for Catholic investigators. Establishing commonalities of truth between the greater mysteries of anthroposophy and the lesser mysteries of the Church concerning the person of Christ-Jesus requires some of the deepest mystery-wisdom of esoteric Christianity.

According to the familiar Catholic understanding of Christ-Jesus, from the moment of Mary's conception —through a miraculous, undescribed process involving the Holy Spirit—the person of God the Son took physical incarnation by hypostatically uniting his divine nature with human nature. Even though Christ-Jesus possessed two distinct natures, he was one person, the person of God the Son.

While this concise dogmatic understanding very succinctly describes *what* occurred with the incarnation of Christ-Jesus, there is no detailed explanation of exactly *how* the infinite and eternal God was able to enter into the finite and temporal universe without being diminished in any way. Or to phrase it more simply: how does almighty God become human on earth and still remain God in heaven? Since the "how" of the miraculous incarnation is outside the purview of Catholic theology, the "what" that occurred therefore requires acceptance by faith.

When examining and evaluating the complex and detailed Christology of anthroposophy, it is best understood as a spiritual-scientific attempt to understand the "how" of Christ-Jesus' incarnation, in a manner similar to physical science's attempt to understand the "how" of natural cosmic events.

Perhaps the best way to begin is with a metaphorical illustration. Visualize the sparkling reflection of the sun in a single dewdrop. In a very real, scientific sense, the tiny reflected point of light is a miniature sun that is directly connected by a continuous beam of light to the great central sun of our planetary system. In a far-transcendent, but analogous way, the human nature of Christ-Jesus is the watery dewdrop on earth, and his divine nature is God's concentrated luminous reflection that is directly connected by a beam of spirituality to the full glory of God the Son in the heavens. Less figuratively speaking, the divine nature of Christ-Jesus is the reflection of the spiritual Son in the mirror of his human nature; and this divine reflection is substantially united to the infinite and eternal God in heaven.

The reflection of the Son in his human nature constitutes the true ego-self—the "I"—of Christ-Jesus; whereby he could truthfully declare: "I AM the Son of God"; and "I and the Father (God) are one."

While this metaphorical illustration does provide a helpful, comprehensive understanding of the hypostatic union of Christ-Jesus, anthroposophical spiritual science goes much deeper. Once again using the image of the sun reflected in a dewdrop, when a beam of sunlight reaches down to the earth from its heavenly source, it must travel through the orbital sphere of Mercury, the orbital sphere of Venus, the orbital sphere of the moon, and then through the earth's enveloping atmosphere in order to reach the terrestrial surface. Analogously, in order to reach the human nature of Christ-Jesus on earth, the divine light of the Son needed to descend through various levels (spheres) of superphysical beings, from seraphim to angels. This hierarchy of celestial beings is also familiar to Catholic theology through the work of St. Thomas

Aquinas (please refer to Figure 4 below).

	WESTERN THEOLOGY	HEBREW TRADITION	GREEK TRADITION	ANTHROPOSOPHY
THE TRIUNE GOD	THE BLESSED TRINITY (INCLUDES)	YAHWEH	THEOS	THE TRINITY
THE WORD	THE WORD	MEMRA	LOGOS	THE CREATIVE WORD
FIRST HIERARCHY	SERAPHIM	CHAIOTH HA-QADESH	(SERAPHIM)	SPIRITS OF LOVE
	CHERUBIM	AUPHANIM	(CHERUBIM)	SPIRITS OF HARMONY
	THRONES	CHASHMALIM	(THRONES)	SPIRITS OF WILL
SECOND HIERARCHY	DOMINIONS	SERAPHIM	KYRIOTETES	SPIRITS OF WISDOM
	VIRTUES	MALACHIM	DYNAMEIS	SPIRITS OF MOVEMENT
	POWERS	ELOHIM	EXUSIAI	SPIRITS OF FORM
THIRD HIERARCHY	PRINCIPALITIES	BENE ELOHIM	ARCHAI	TIME SPIRITS
	ARCHANGELS	KERUBIM	ARCHANGELOI	SUN SPIRITS
	ANGELS	ISHIM	ANGELOI	MOON SPIRITS
	HUMANITY	BENEI-ADAM	ANTHROPOS	SPIRITS OF FREEDOM

Figure 4: The Universal Hierarchy of Being

According to anthroposophical spiritual science, however, this downward descent of the light of the Son through the celestial hierarchy was abbreviated, abridged and expedited by the compassionate and selfless intermediation of a highly-advanced archangelic being. Due to his advanced development, this archangelic being was able to function at the level of a virtue; and thereby assume the leadership of the exalted beings who superphysically inhabit our sun. Throughout history, this great regent of the sun has been known by various names: Vishva-Karman, Ahura Mazdao and Osirus. In the ancient Greek mysteries, this "spirit of truth" who was to descend to the earth as the saviour of humanity was known as "Christos." In esoteric Christianity, the majestic sun-king is called the "Solar-Christos."

Since his highest vehicles of expression reached up to the universal love principle of the Logos-Word,[33] and his lowest range of influence extended to the level of the astral body, the Solar-Christos could act as a super-celestial bridge between the man Jesus and the divine person of the Son. The Solar-Christos was able to accomplish this intermediation by sacrificially indwelling and permeating the body and soul of a specially-prepared human being.

According to spiritual science, the man Jesus was a unique soul in human history. During the ancient Lemurian Age, prior to the Luciferic corruption of humanity that resulted in the "fall" from superphysical paradise (that is, original sin), this nascent ego-soul was protected and preserved by powerful celestial beings (Elohim) in an etheric, angel-like condition. As such, he is esoterically known as the "heavenly-Adam" or "Lord Immanuel."

Since the Immanuel-soul had no prior incarnations before his birth as Jesus, his nativity in Bethlehem was truly a "virgin birth" free from original sin. Later, in his twelfth year, the already exceptional soul of Jesus-Immanuel was indwelt and permeated by the ego-forces of a highly-advanced initiate who was once incarnated as Zarathustra, the founder of an ancient Persian religion. The indwelling influence of the Zarathustra-individuality until the thirtieth year of life was of immense benefit in maturing the virginal ego-soul and bodily vehicles (physical, etheric and astral) of Jesus-Immanuel.

Immediately prior to the baptism in the Jordan, the Zarathustra-soul withdrew his indwelling ego-influence from Jesus-Immanuel, to be replaced by the glorious ego-indwelling of the Solar-Christos instead. Through this sublime indwelling, the consciousness of Jesus-Immanuel was raised and expanded to the level of the Logos-Word, thereby establishing a supernal conduit for the powerful downpouring of divine love directly from God the Son. According to spiritual science, then, Jesus-Immanuel became Jesus the Christ (or Messiah)—the son of God—at the baptism.

At the baptism, then, the human nature of Jesus-Immanuel was hypostatically united to the divine nature of God the Son through the intermediary connection of the Solar-Christos with the Logos-Word (please refer to Figure 5 on the following page).

From this more complicated esoteric Christology, it is mistakenly easy to conclude that the person of Christ-Jesus is a combination of beings; or if he is a single person, which person is he—Jesus-Immanuel, the Solar-Christos, the Logos-Word or God the Son? Since most anthroposophists have only a vague and limited understanding of the Logos-Word and of God the Son, and since they tend to forget or ignore the being of Jesus-Immanuel (aka: the "Nathan-Jesus"), they have mistakenly concluded that the person of Christ-Jesus is simply the Solar-Christos (aka: the "Christ-being").

In the case of Catholic Christology, though Christ-Jesus is mistakenly equated with the Logos-Word (the "Universal Man," or "Adam-Kadmon"), it is correct in infallibly declaring that Christ-Jesus is one person—the divine person of God the Son.

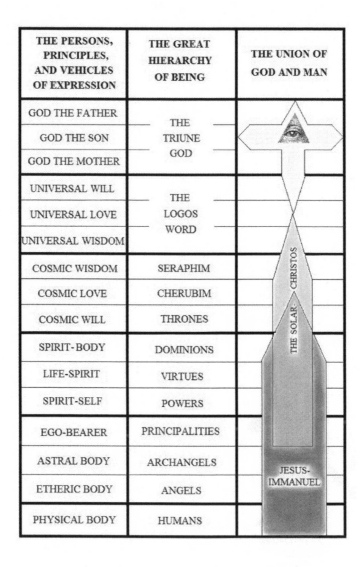

THE PERSONS, PRINCIPLES, AND VEHICLES OF EXPRESSION	THE GREAT HIERARCHY OF BEING	THE UNION OF GOD AND MAN
GOD THE FATHER	THE TRIUNE GOD	
GOD THE SON		
GOD THE MOTHER		
UNIVERSAL WILL	THE LOGOS WORD	
UNIVERSAL LOVE		
UNIVERSAL WISDOM		
COSMIC WISDOM	SERAPHIM	
COSMIC LOVE	CHERUBIM	
COSMIC WILL	THRONES	
SPIRIT-BODY	DOMINIONS	
LIFE-SPIRIT	VIRTUES	
SPIRIT-SELF	POWERS	
EGO-BEARER	PRINCIPALITIES	
ASTRAL BODY	ARCHANGELS	
ETHERIC BODY	ANGELS	
PHYSICAL BODY	HUMANS	

Figure 5: The Hypostatic Union of God and Man

The confusion about how "the man Jesus" is not a "human person," but rather a "divine person," is due primarily to a lack of understanding about the mystical process of "lawful indwelling." In lawful indwelling, a more advanced being is able to temporarily permeate and influence the body and soul vehicles of another being that is less advanced. Unlike "unlawful possession," the indwelling entity has free-will permission and cooperation to do so, and does not in any way decrease, minimize or replace the ego-awareness of the other being. Instead, the consciousness and ego-awareness of the indwelt individual becomes temporarily raised and enhanced to the superior level of the more advanced being. When the indwelling presence is withdrawn, the indwelt individual returns to their normal conscious awareness, but retains the memory of their enlightening experience.

In this way throughout history, humanity has been beneficially influenced and guided by angels, archangels, bodhisattvas, buddhas, folk-spirits and other advanced beings.

In the case of "the man Jesus" (that is, Jesus-Immanuel) at the baptism, the indwelling presence of the Solar-Christos (the "Christ-being") powerfully raised and expanded his own ego-awareness (his own "I-self") to the supernal level of the Logos-Word. At this level of cosmic consciousness, the Son is better able to gloriously reflect his full divine being and personhood. In other words, with the exalted consciousness provided by the indwelling Solar-Christos, Jesus-Immanuel fully experienced and realized that his true ego-self, his true personhood, his true "I," was a direct reflection of God the Son.

In very truth, then, through the cosmic consciousness of the Logos-Word, all individual ego-awareness merges and unites with the "I" of the Son; that is, one's individual personhood transcendently expands and deepens to become one with the personhood of the divine Son. The true personhood of Christ-Jesus, then, is the person of the divine

Son.

According to esoteric Christianity, Jesus-Immanuel was the first human "person" (ego-being) to consciously unite with the "person" (divine-being) of God the Son. As such, he became "the messiah," the saviour of mankind who would overcome sin, sickness, evil and death through the power of divine love. By overcoming these afflictions in his own life, he provided mankind with "the way" to do likewise; and thereby unite with God the Son as well.

In order to continue being the salvational conduit for the transformative power of divine love from the Son, the Solar-Christos must continue to indwell Jesus-Immanuel until "the end of the age" (Matt 28:20). To tether his nature and destiny to the slow redemption of mankind and the earth for thousands of years to come is, one would agree, an incomprehensible self-sacrifice for such an exalted being who's true superphysical home is the sun. Truly, mankind already owes a huge debt of gratitude to the selfless and compassionate devotedness of the Christ-being. Moreover, it is obvious to esoteric reflection that the benevolent actions of the Solar-Christos are also impulses of divine love issuing from the very heart of the divine Son.

No doubt most Catholics will find the preceding esoteric Christology much too novel, complex and difficult to comprehend.[34] It is for those individuals that the lesser mysteries of exoteric Christianity are directed. In the same way that most people have no interest in learning integral calculus; but instead, are quite content just to learn the basic operations of simple arithmetic (addition, subtraction, multiplication and division), most Catholics are quite content and prefer the more abbreviated religious truth contained in Church dogma.

Moreover, in the same way that the Catholic Church, as a religious institution, is not compelled to unquestioning accept the theories of natural science (such as cosmic worm-holes, dark matter, Darwinism or general relativity), it is also not compelled to immediately embrace and incorporate the research results of anthroposophical spiritual science either. Nevertheless, the Church does have the freedom and authority to accept scientific ideas—that don't contradict the already-declared infallible truths—if it so chooses.

In the case of anthroposophy, since it is an authentic science (albeit of the spirit), it cannot accept religious truth simply on the basis of Church authority. It is compelled by the requirements of its discipline to independently and objectively test and examine any and all declarations of truth for itself. Therefore, even though it must test and examine the declared truths of Catholicism, very often those dogmatic truths have been validated by independent, spiritual-scientific investigation.

In the area of Christology, then, even though it is understood that the lesser mysteries (the infallible truths) of the exoteric Church cannot incorporate the deep complexity of the greater mysteries, it should still be obvious to sincere Church authorities that anthroposophy does not pose a threat to Church doctrine, any more than the natural sciences. In fact, some open-minded theologians might even recognize that anthroposophical spiritual science is actually a valuable spiritual ally in opposing the modernist forces of materialism, naturalism, atheism, secularism, relativism, Darwinism and scientism.

8.5 Reconciling the Doctrine of Repeated Lives with Catholic Theology

Another area of anthroposophical investigation—that is even more foreign to traditional Catholic teaching than esoteric Christology—is the doctrine of repeated lives. According to Catholic theology:

The Church teaches that every spiritual soul is created immediately by God—it is not "produced" by the parents—and also that it is immortal: it does not perish when it separates from the body at death, and it will be reunited with the body at the final Resurrection. (Paragraph 366; *Catechism of the Catholic Church*)

The Church, then, asserts that even though the immortal human soul can exist without the body after death, it had no incorporeal existence prior to conception. Therefore, even though the human soul is believed to experience only one existence in a physical body that is subject to death, it is also believed that the postmortem soul will miraculously re-inhabit the discarded (but "resurrected") physical body sometime in the future. In this sense, then, Church doctrine does acknowledge a single "re-incarnation" of the human soul.

Catholic teaching also asserts that human souls first began to inhabit bodies subject to death only after the commission of original sin (that is, the initial disobedience to God), and the consequent expulsion from paradise. Previous to this, our primal ancestors are believed to have inhabited immortal bodies that weren't subject to illness, infirmity, old-age and death.[35]

While the investigations of spiritual science fully agree with much of the Catholic teaching here described, there are, however, some noteworthy areas of difference. For example, spiritual science asserts that *all* human souls—not just our parental ancestors—were differentiated from the substance of the Elohim (refer to Figure 4, if necessary) prior to the Luciferic corruption that resulted in the "fall" from paradise. Moreover, this "fall" is understood to mean a gradual coarsening and materialization of the once invisible and ethereal human body. This descent into coarse materiality resulted in the once-immortal human form becoming increasingly subject to illness, infirmity, old-age and death.

As a result of the progressive deterioration of the human body, the immortal soul needed to vacate the worn-out vehicle of expression, and re-inhabit a new one in order to continue its destined evolution on earth. Differing in this respect from Catholic belief, spiritual science maintains that the soul's full potential on earth requires more than just one lifetime to achieve. Believing that the immortal human soul will spend a blissful eternity in heaven or a tormented eternity in hell entirely on the basis of one single lifetime strikes most discerning thinkers as prohibitively unreasonable. Moreover, having only one chance at heaven seems awfully unfair, since every soul is born into a broad range of differing conditions: one soul may be born healthy and talented into a well-respected, wealthy family; while another soul may be born talentless into abject poverty as an orphan with severe physical and mental handicaps.

Nevertheless, spiritual science does not in any way fault the Catholic Church for historically maintaining and promoting the belief in only one life on earth for every human soul. Anthroposophical research recognizes that, for the past two thousand years, the widely-accepted belief in a single lifetime was entirely necessary in order to direct Euro-American cultural development toward the technological mastery of the physical world. As expressed by Rudolf Steiner in an answer session that followed a lecture given on 3 February 1907:

> To develop civilization, human beings had to come to love the earth; they had to be cut off from their earlier incarnations and love only the one in which they were at the time. The whole of humanity once had to go through a period when they knew nothing of their higher principles and of earlier incarnations. Christianity did not teach reincarnation in public for two millennia ...

By contrast, in Eastern cultures (such ,as India) where a

belief in multiple lives has historically prevailed, technological progress was stifled and delayed for several centuries. Human laziness being what it is, those who believe they have more than one life to live are more likely to avoid painful or unpleasant tasks until a later lifetime; thereby delaying their present necessary development.

During the last two thousand years, esoteric Christianity has also been publicly silent regarding the doctrine of repeated lives. Even though the doctrine was secretly known, it was never openly revealed by either the Knights of the Holy Grail or the Fraternity of the Rose Cross. This strict esoteric enforcement was in keeping with a direct request from Christ-Jesus immediately following his transfiguration on Mount Tabor. During that event, Christ-Jesus revealed to his three most-advanced disciples, Peter, James and John, that the prophet Elijah was reborn as John the baptist. As biblically described in Matthew (17:10–13):

> And the disciples asked him, "Then why do the scribes say that first Elijah must come?" He replied, "Elijah does come, and he is to restore all things; but I tell you that Elijah has already come, and they did not know him, but did to him whatever they pleased. So also the Son of man will suffer at their hands." Then the disciples understood that he was speaking to them of John the Baptist.

Furthermore, the biblical passage that states: "And as they were coming down the mountain, Jesus commanded them, "Tell no one the vision, until the Son of man is raised from the dead" (Matt 17:9) is understood and interpreted by spiritual science to mean that Christ-Jesus personally instructed his three inmost disciples[36] to not teach the truth of repeated lives until a future time when he will begin to reappear in his resurrected form. Since Christ-Jesus began to increasingly appear throughout the world in his resurrected etheric form at the beginning of the twentieth century, the doctrine of repeated lives can rightfully begin to be publicly revealed to Western cultures in a beneficial way. Western cultures have certainly gained scientific and technological mastery over physical nature during the past two thousand years; so now it is crucially important to direct investigative attention back to the spiritual world, or risk becoming forever enmeshed in deadening materialism.

Since esoteric Christianity (in this case, the Rosicrucian Fraternity) has known and safeguarded Western mystery-knowledge of repeated lives since the thirteenth century, it is not surprising that anthroposophy—and not the Catholic Church—would be the first, world-wide Christian institution to publicly disseminate this once hidden information. And because the Church of St. Peter is singularly focused on maintaining and promulgating the lesser mysteries of Christ-Jesus, it would certainly be unreasonable to expect the Church to suddenly embrace the greater mysteries of repeated lives after two thousand years of maintaining otherwise. But since it can be reasonably argued from scripture that Christ-Jesus shared the truth of repeated lives with his closest disciples, it is very likely that the Church at some point in the future will also openly declare this age-old truth.

When present-day esoteric Christianity (anthroposophy) does convey information about repeated lives, it tries to avoid using the word, "reincarnation." This is because the term is almost always popularly misunderstood; as well as because it can mean quite different things to different religions. For example, in Hinduism it is believed that the human soul ("atman") is immortal; and that after death it immediately incarnates in another form, including animals, demons and divinities. In Buddhism, however, it is believed that human beings have no immortal soul; but that immediately after death, one's former consciousness passes into another body, which also includes animals.

The spiritual science of anthroposophy completely rejects

the erroneous and harmful notion that human souls can reincarnate into animal bodies. Even though ancestral humanity went through an animal-like stage of evolution prior to receiving an individuated soul during the ancient Lemurian Age, discarnate human souls only re-inhabit human bodies. Moreover, spiritual-scientific investigation also contends that human souls after death do not immediately re-inhabit new bodies; but instead, they spend variable periods of time in the spiritual world reviewing their previous life-experience, and preparing for the next appropriate rebirth. The life-circumstances of a subsequent rebirth are perceived to be determined by the moral actions, personal decisions, religious inclinations, interpersonal relations and lifestyle choices that were enacted during the previous incarnation.[37]

While the human soul is recognized as being immortal, anthroposophy and Catholicism both agree that it is not immutable; that is, the human soul is verifiably subject to change (both positive and negative). As a result, prior to each incarnation, the soul is created anew—with new talents, new abilities, new inclinations, new strengths, new weaknesses, new fears, new opportunities, new ambitions, new parents, new relatives, new birthplace, new birthdate and renewed vitality.

Furthermore, anthroposophical research agrees with Church teaching that at some time in the future, Christ-imbued human beings will no longer incarnate into bodies of coarse earthly matter; but will instead inhabit angel-like "resurrection" bodies that are once again incorruptible.

Hopefully at this point it will be clear to Catholic critics that anthroposophy does not in any way endorse the erroneous Eastern notions of reincarnation. Moreover, anthroposophy sincerely believes that the public promulgation of repeated lives that began in the early-twentieth century is in accordance with the salvational intentions of Christ-Jesus.

CONCLUSION

The Slow Befriending of Anthroposophy and Catholicism in Our Time

EVEN THOUGH FEW present-day anthroposophists and few current Catholics recognize and understand the two-millennial division of Christian teaching into exoteric mystery-wisdom and esoteric mystery-wisdom, there are still noteworthy examples in recent years which show that each side is beginning to amicably learn more about the other.

Even though the anthroposophical leadership in Dornach, Switzerland does not officially converse with the Catholic Church, and even though the Vatican Curia in Rome does not officially converse with the General Anthroposophical Society, individual anthroposophists and Catholics have begun to slowly befriend each other.

It will probably come as a complete shock and surprise, to both anthroposophists and Catholics alike, to discover that Karol Josef Wojtyla (1920–2005)—before he became Pope John Paul II—was involved with an anthroposophical group in Poland that was studying the art of speech and working with Rudolf Steiner's mystery dramas. Moreover, before he became Pope Benedict XVI, Cardinal Joseph Ratzinger (b.1927) was the head (or "prefect") of the Congregation for the Doctrine of the Faith from 1981 to 2005. In this capacity (where he was nicknamed, "God's Rottweiler"), Cardinal Ratzinger's primary function was to defend and reaffirm traditional Catholic doctrine. During that time, he was friends with Dr. Martin Kriele (b.1931), a well-respected German constitutional lawyer who was both Catholic and anthroposophist. In an interview given in 1988, Kriele stated:

> I don't withhold [from the Catholic Church] that I'm an anthroposophist and I must say that it's caused me not the slightest difficulty and even the ultimate arbiter [of the Church], so to speak, Cardinal Ratzinger, knows me to be an anthroposophist. He is today the ultimate defender of the faith and he took no offense from that.

Moreover, in Kriele's experience, Catholics were much more accepting of him being an anthroposophist, than anthroposophists were of him being a Catholic.[38] As he indicated in the same interview quoted above:

> Catholicism, meanwhile, has become much more open. It's often happened to me that my coreligionists respond not with hostility but with interest when I say that I am an anthroposophist. When, among anthroposophists, I mention that I am a Catholic, however, they act like they are about to cross themselves [as protection from the devil].

In Kriele's opinion, this fearful and widespread anti-Catholic reaction among anthroposophists is misplaced and anachronistic. As he explained:

> It seems to me that those who behave thus are seeing the reality around them not through their own eyes but through those of Rudolf Steiner seventy years hence. Not quite of course—Steiner himself had positive relations with Catholics. He even on January 30th, 1924—after the

114

Christmas meeting!—went as far as to say that the Catholic church is the only important institution that truly presents to the world the mystery of the spirit that has veiled itself with sensory impressions (*Mystery Centres of the Middle Ages*; GA 233a); awareness of its role, however, usually being absent ... Anthroposophists who orient themselves only by Steiner's explanations of forms of Catholicism of his own time and ignore his favorable expressions mistake the present reality; for example, that the church today recognizes religious freedom as an inalienable right, for other religions as much as itself. Further, supremacy of the conscience over dogma is now officially taught and also that departure from the church need not rank one among unbelievers. (Ibid.)

While John Paul II and Benedict XVI are certainly two examples of celebrated Catholics who have had an arm's-length brush with anthroposophy, many other ordinary Catholics have also had similar favourable associations. For example, many Catholic parents have positively enrolled their children in anthroposophically-inspired Waldorf schools, or Camphill communities. Other Catholics have been pleasantly involved with anthroposophically-inspired Biodynamic farming; while others have enjoyably attended anthroposophically-inspired eurythmy performances or Mystery plays.

In other instances, some Catholics in recent years have deliberately delved much deeper into the anthroposophical material of Rudolf Steiner. During the early 1990s, for instance, Vatican scholars at the Institute for Philosophy in Liechtenstein (a Catholic research centre) studied Rudolf Steiner as an eminent spiritual philosopher, and concluded that anthroposophy was reasonably harmonious with accepted Catholic doctrine.

So, has there been a reciprocal interest on the part of anthroposophical groups to study Catholic doctrine and teaching? There doesn't appear so—but in fairness, it is much more difficult to study a religion than it is to study a science (including a spiritual one). Religion requires emotional commitment, dedicated devotion, communal activity and repeated practice. A science, on the other hand, can be more easily understood in an objective, intellectual way. So for anthroposophists to truly understand Catholicism, they would actually have to practice or apply it for a certain length of time. Nevertheless, present-day anthroposophists can still achieve a much deeper understanding and appreciation of today's Catholicism just by having Catholic speakers and experts attend anthroposophical group meetings; or by personally attending and observing a Christmas or Easter Mass.

Since the very beginning of anthroposophy, there has always been a small percentage of Catholics involved. One of the founding teachers of the first Waldorf school, for example, was Dr. Karl Schubert (1889–1949), a Catholic anthroposophist that Rudolf Steiner held in high esteem. Even at the Christmas Conference in 1923, when the General Anthroposophical Society was officially established, Rudolf Steiner was accompanied by a Catholic priest named Father Trinquero.

Throughout the history of anthroposophy, most Catholic members have preferred to quietly practice their religious faith without widespread Society attention or notice. Moreover, they have generally preferred to keep these two areas of their lives separate, without making public efforts to unite or integrate them. There have been, of course, a few exceptions by some present-day anthroposophists who are favorably disposed to Catholicism. Prominent anthroposophical writers, Robert A. Powell (b.1947) and Christopher Bamford, for instance, have attempted to imitate the Catholic veneration of the Blessed Virgin Mary by instituting the "Hermetic" celebration of the "Virgin

Sophia"—the Holy Spirit of Wisdom.

Unfortunately, Powell, Bamford and other like-minded Catholic supporters within anthroposophy have been vocal champions of Valentin Tomberg, the controversial anthroposophical convert to Catholicism (please refer to Chapter 5 for more detail). Not surprisingly, then, those anthroposophists who regard Valentin Tomberg with suspicion and derision very often regard the Catholic-friendly "Tombergians" within anthroposophy with equal suspicion and wariness. Many members have also mistakenly concluded that all Catholic anthroposophists are Tomberg supporters; and this quite naturally raises questions about Catholic inclusion.

Clearly the lesson to be learned from the continuing Tombergian divisiveness is that efforts to interfuse and amalgamate anthroposophy and Catholicism (even well-intentioned efforts) are unhealthy, unproductive and mutually ruinous. Not just institutionally, but even within the sanctity of our own souls, it is vitally important to maintain a healthy autonomy between the religion of Catholicism and the (spiritual) science of anthroposophy. By doing so, these two crucial streams of Christian mystery-teaching will truly complement and elevate each other, now and into the future.

NOTES

CHAPTER 2

1. The Feast of Corpus Christi ("Body of Christ") is an annual celebration in the Catholic calendar that occurs on the first Thursday after Trinity Sunday (the first Sunday after Pentecost). The feast celebrates the sacrament of Holy Communion—the transubstantiated body and blood of Christ-Jesus. Traditionally, a public procession is enacted with the consecrated host (the sacramental bread) on display in an ornamental receptacle called a "monstrance."

2. When Rudolf Steiner was nine years old, he supersensibly perceived a distant aunt who (unbeknown to the rest of his family) had recently died.

3. Popularized by the influence of St. Bernard of Clairvaux, the Order of Cistercians (or "White Monks") are a strict monastic offshoot of the Benedictine Order. Throughout the Middle Ages and Renaissance centuries, the Cistercians were responsible for spreading technological advances in agriculture, hydraulic engineering and metallurgy. In the post-Renaissance period, they became more active in education and academic pursuits.

CHAPTER 3

4. In the Publisher's Preface of *The Case of Valentin Tomberg* (Sergei O. Prokofieff; 1997) an important clarification has been helpfully provided to correct any misconception that Rudolf Steiner was "anti-Catholic" in his criticisms of the Church. It states as follows:

    > When Rudolf Steiner speaks of malevolently retrogressive elements with Roman Catholicism, he is referring to small numbers of individuals who, as 'initiates', are consciously involved in steering humanity in a particular course. (The vast majority of ordinary Catholics—and even Jesuits—are not implicated in such plans.) ... [T]hese 'initiates' within the Church wish to hold humanity back in its development to the stage of the 'intellectual soul', rather than allowing it to progress to the present 'consciousness soul' epoch. During the intellectual soul stage of evolution, the structure, hierarchical form and fixed teachings of the established Roman Church were suitable for an adolescent human consciousness, whereas now a spirituality based on 'ethical individualism'—individual freedom and responsibility arising from personal conscience—is a more appropriate (and Christian) ideal. (This is not to say, however, that the Christian Sacraments as practiced in the Catholic Church are not necessary today.)

5. Concerning this scriptural passage, the *Catechism of the Catholic Church* offers the following explanation:

    > Sometimes the soul is distinguished from the spirit: St. Paul for instance prays that God may sanctify his people "wholly," with "spirit and soul and body" kept sound and blameless at the Lord's coming. The

Church teaches that this distinction does not introduce a duality into the soul. "Spirit" signifies that from creation man is ordered to a supernatural end and that his soul can gratuitously be raised beyond all it deserves to communion with God. (Paragraph 367)

CHAPTER 4

6. No doubt, President Bill Clinton's famously specious remark: "I did not have sexual relations with that woman, Miss Lewinsky," was a perfect example of Jesuit "casuistry" that he learned as a graduate of Georgetown University. He later claimed that this statement wasn't a lie because (in his own mind) he defined "sexual relations" only as "sexual intercourse" (which he hadn't performed), and not "oral sex and masturbation" (which he had engaged in).

7. The Ignatian *Spiritual Exercises* are not just exclusively used in training Jesuit candidates. Various versions of these exercises are also offered to non-members in Jesuit-led workshops, lectures and retreats.

CHAPTER 5

8. As a highly-trained esotericist and clairvoyant himself, Rudolf Steiner strongly advised that one should not step forward as a serious teacher of esotericism before the age of forty. Without the required developmental maturity, serious errors in supersensible instruction are likely to occur. Tomberg clearly ignored his teacher's sage advice and began his own anthroposophically-oriented writing and lecturing when he was only thirty.

9. One iconic example of an extremist personality was Jerry

Rubin (1938–1994) who went from being a rabid anti-establishment, social-activist Yippie in the 1960s and 1970s; to being a multimillionaire, capitalist stockbroker Yuppie in the 1980s.

10. Though von Balthasar became a Jesuit in 1929, he was forced to leave the Order in 1950 in order to continue his mystically-oriented pursuits in connection with the Johannine Community (a secular institute he co-founded in 1945 with a converted mystic and stigmatist, Adrienne von Speyr). In consequence of leaving his religious order, the Congregation for Seminaries and Universities imposed a teaching ban on von Balthasar.

One specific example of von Balthasar's heretical notions is found in a deliberately provocative 1950s essay entitled, "Casta Meretrix" ("Chaste Harlot"). In this essay, he shockingly maintains that "the prostitute" (the Great Harlot) is a positive symbol for the Church:

> The figure of the prostitute is so appropriate for the Church ... that it ... defines the Church of the New Covenant in her most splendid mystery of salvation.

This idea hardly complies with the orthodox position that "The Church is the spotless bride of the spotless Lamb" (Paragraph 796 of the *Catechism of the Catholic Church*).

11. Any reader sincerely wanting to know more about authentic Hermeticism and not the pseudo-version championed by Tomberg is referred to *The Kybalion: A Study of the Hermetic Philosophy of Ancient Egypt and Greece* by Three Initiates (2013).

12. Tomberg openly celebrated the occult influencing of his tarot meditations. On page 4 he stated: "the Major Arcana of the Tarot are authentic symbols, i.e. they are "magic ... operations."

CHAPTER 6

13. Our own cultural era has also been esoterically termed, the "Anglo-Saxon Teutonic" era. Since we are currently living in this particular era and do not wish to offend other, non-Western European cultures, esoteric Christianity often uses the designation, "fifth post-Atlantean" cultural era. Nevertheless, even on the basis of casual observation—for example, the cross-cultural ubiquity of the business suit and tie, as well as the universality of the English language—the world-wide influence of Western European culture is clearly evident.

Some observers might object that American culture is even more pervasive. But from an esoteric point of view, the United States (and other countries such as Canada and Australia) are simply considered colonial offshoots of Western European culture that share the same basic cultural impulses as their parent nations.

14. While the vast majority of Catholic believers throughout the Middle Ages were quite content to accept religious truth strictly on the basis of Church authority, the more advanced theological thinkers (such as Scholastic philosopher, St. Thomas Aquinas) were well aware that "appeal to authority" was one of the weakest of all philosophical arguments for truth.

CHAPTER 7

15. The teaching authority of the Catholic Church is termed the "magisterium," and is a decision-making assembly comprised of the pope in communion with all the world-bishops. The magisterium has the authority to establish Church dogma.

16. The wording of the "Nicene Creed" is as follows:

I believe in one God, the Father, the Almighty, maker of heaven and earth, of all things visible and invisible. I believe in one Lord Jesus Christ, the only begotten Son of God; born of the Father before all ages; God from God, Light from Light, true God from true God; begotten, not made, consubstantial with the Father; through him all things were made.

For us men and for our salvation he came down from heaven: and by the Holy Spirit was incarnate of the Virgin Mary, and became man.

For our sake he was crucified under Pontius Pilate; he suffered death and was buried, and rose again on the third day, in accordance with the Scriptures. He ascended into heaven and is seated at the right hand of the Father. He will come again in glory to judge the living and the dead, and his kingdom will have no end.

I believe in the Holy Spirit, the Lord, the giver of life, who proceeds from the Father and the Son; who with the Father and the Son is adored and glorified; who has spoken through the Prophets.

I believe in one, holy, catholic, and apostolic Church. I confess one baptism for the forgiveness of sins, and I look forward to the resurrection of the dead, and the life of the world to come. Amen.

17. The wording of the "Apostles' Creed" is as follows:

I believe in God, the Father almighty, creator of heaven and earth; and in Jesus Christ, his only Son our Lord; who was conceived by the Holy Spirit, born of the Virgin Mary, suffered under Pontius Pilate, was crucified, died, and was buried.

He descended into hell; on the third day he rose again from the dead; he ascended into heaven, and is seated at the right hand of God, the Father almighty; from there he will come to judge the living and the dead.

I believe in the Holy Spirit, the holy catholic Church, the communion of saints, the forgiveness of sins, the resurrection of the body and life everlasting. Amen.

18. In a sort of comic irony, Rudolf Steiner stated that in the late 1800s, this widespread emphasis on the completely unfettered freedom of thought was itself a kind of dogma:

> At the beginning of the last third of the Nineteenth Century the belief prevailed among educated people that the human being ought to form his own convictions out of his own self ... There was, so to say, a kind of dogma, but a dogma freely recognized in the widest circles, that, among people who had reached a certain degree of culture, freedom of conscience was possible. (From a lecture given on 30 May 1920, entitled "Roman Catholicism")

19. Basically understood, "humanism" is a system of thought that considers human beings to be intrinsically good, and that human progress is best determined by intellectual reason, rather than religious dogma and belief.

20. "Rationalism," simply stated, is the philosophical belief that intellectual reason and experience are superior to emotion and religious belief in determining knowledge and truth.

21. "Darwinism" is a theory of biological evolution developed by Charles Darwin (1809–1882) which asserts that the development and change of all living organisms is due entirely to random mutation and natural selection. As such, there are no supernatural or spiritual forces involved or required.

22. "Naturalism" is the philosophical belief that only natural laws and forces exist and operate in the world. According to naturalism, supernatural laws and forces do not exist or operate.

23. "Materialism" is the ideological position that matter is the fundamental basis of everything in nature; and therefore, there is nothing spiritual (non-material) or supernatural that exists.

24. "Relativism" is the belief that there is no absolute truth or validity in nature. All points of view are equally valid, and all truth is subjectively relative to the individual.

25. "Communism" is a materialistic, social ideology that asserts that economic forces are the sole determining factors in human society. Religious belief is considered to be an illusion and a crutch that needs to be abolished for true human happiness to occur.

26. "Futurism" was an artistic and social movement of the early-twentieth century that glorified and celebrated speed technology (such as cars and planes) and urban modernity. The past was rejected by futurism as a stifling weight to human progress.

27. "Scientism" is the belief that the scientific method is the only reliable way of acquiring knowledge and understanding of the world. All other avenues of pursuit, such as religion and philosophy, are dismissed.

28. "Secularism" is the ideological assertion that a healthy society requires a "separation of church and state"; that is, religious belief should not unduly influence governmental decisions, and government legislation should not unduly influence religious practice and belief. Unfortunately, secularism can also serve as a justification for atheistic politicians to isolate and marginalize various religions from the rest of society.

29. Even though Steiner made numerous criticisms regarding the nineteenth-century Catholic Church's lack of

intellectual freedom, in a few other instances he did acknowledge that the Church has the innate potential for tremendous inner freedom:

> There were always certain clergy who worked to bring about a certain freedom in Catholicism. I say quite frankly that in the sixties of the nineteenth century in a large number of the Catholic clergy seeds of development of the Catholic principle were present which, if they had passed over into a free science, might in large measure have led to a liberation of modern humanity ...

> [T]he freest of all churches ... for in its essential nature the Catholic Church is capable of the greatest freedom. You will perhaps be astonished that I should say that. (From "Roman Catholicism": 30 May 1920)

CHAPTER 8

30. The notion of compatibility between reason and faith, scientific truth and religious truth, has long been affirmed by the Catholic Church. As stated in Paragraph 159 of the *Catechism of the Catholic Church*:

> *Faith and science*: "Though faith is above reason, there can never be any real discrepancy between faith and reason. Since the same God who reveals mysteries and infuses faith has bestowed the light of reason on the human mind, God cannot deny himself, nor can truth ever contradict truth." "Consequently, methodical research in all branches of knowledge, provided it is carried out in a truly scientific manner and does not override moral laws, can never conflict with the faith, because the things of the world and the

things of faith derive from the same God. The humble and persevering investigator of the secrets of nature is being led, as it were, by the hand of God in spite of himself, for it is God, the conserver of all things, who made them what they are."

31. As stated in Paragraph 375 of the *Catechism of the Catholic Church*:

> The Church, interpreting the symbolism of biblical language in an authentic way, in the light of the New Testament and Tradition, teaches that our first parents, Adam and Eve, were constituted in an original "state of holiness and justice."

32. Christology is an area of study within Christian theology that examines the nature and person of Christ-Jesus, such as the hypostatic union of his humanity and his divinity.

33. For a more detailed esoteric Christian understanding of the Logos-Word, please refer to my own publication: *The Greater Mysteries of the Divine Trinity, the Logos-Word and Creation* (available from Amazon.com; 2015).

34. For those individuals who do wish to deepen their understanding of anthroposophical Christology, Rudolf Steiner's *From Jesus to Christ* (Rudolf Steiner Press; 2005), *The Gospel of Saint Luke* (SteinerBooks; 1990) and *The Christian Mystery* (Completion Press; 2000) are all highly recommended. My own book, *The Star of Higher Knowledge: The Five Guiding Mysteries of Esoteric Christianity* (available from Amazon.com; 2015) may also prove helpful.

35. The biblical passage in Genesis (3:21, 23) that states: "And the LORD God made for Adam and for his wife garments of skins, and clothed them ... therefore the LORD God sent him forth from the garden of Eden" is esoterically understood to mean that mankind began to inhabit bodies of skin, flesh and blood only *after* the expulsion from "paradise" (the superphysical world).

36. Our Saviour's admonition would apply particularly to St. Peter, who would later institute the path of exoteric Christianity; and to St. John (the evangelist) who would later institute the path of esoteric Christianity.

37. For more detailed spiritual-scientific information on the doctrine of repeated lives, Rudolf Steiner's series of lectures published in *Life Between Death and Rebirth* (Anthroposophic Press; 1989) is an excellent place to start.

38. Author's Note: As a Catholic anthroposophist as well, this has also been my own personal experience. Sadly, this reaction is entirely contrary to the open-minded, free-thinking spirit of anthroposophy as envisioned by Rudolf Steiner. Moreover, religious freedom is one of the foundational principles of the General Anthroposophical Society, as stated in point 4:

> The Anthroposophical Society is in no sense a secret society, but is entirely public. Anyone can become a member, without regard to nationality, social standing, religion, scientific or artistic conviction, who considers as justified the existence of an institution such as the Goetheanum in Dornach, in its capacity as a School of Spiritual Science. The Anthroposophical Society rejects any kind of sectarian activity. Party politics it considers not to be within its task.

SELECT BIBLIOGRAPHY

(in alphabetical order)

- *Catechism of the Catholic Church* (Our Sunday Visitor, Publishing Division, 2000)

- Dietrich von Hildebrand, *Transformation in Christ: On the Christian Attitude* (Ignatius Press, 2001)

- Holy Bible, *RSV-CE* (Ignatius Press, 2006)

- Ron MacFarlane, *The Greater Mysteries of the Divine Trinity, the Logos-Word and Creation* (Greater Mysteries Publications, 2015)

- Ron MacFarlane, *The Star of Higher Knowledge: The Five Guiding Mysteries of Esoteric Christianity* (Greater Mysteries Publications, 2015)

- Rudolf Steiner, *An Outline of Esoteric Science* (SteinerBooks, 1997)

- Rudolf Steiner, *From Jesus to Christ* (Rudolf Steiner Press, 1973)

- Rudolf Steiner, *Life Between Death and Rebirth* (Anthroposophic Press, 1978)

- Rudolf Steiner, *Spiritual Hierarchies and their Reflection in the Physical World* (Anthroposophic Press, 1970)

- Rudolf Steiner, *The Christian Mystery* (SteinerBooks, 1998)

- Rudolf Steiner, *The Course of My Life* (Anthroposophic Press, 1970)

- Rudolf Steiner, *The Gospel of St. Luke* (SteinerBooks, 1990)

- Rudolf Steiner, *The Gospel of St. Matthew* (Kessinger Publishing, 2003)

- Rudolf Steiner, *Theosophy* (SteinerBooks, 1994)

- Rudolf Steiner, *The Principle of Spiritual Economy* (Anthroposophic Press, 1986)

- Rudolf Steiner, *The Reappearance of Christ in the Etheric* (SteinerBooks, 2003)

- Three Initiates, *The Kybalion: A Study of the Hermetic Philosophy of Ancient Egypt and Greece* (Merchant Books, 2013)

OTHER BOOKS BY

RON MACFARLANE

THERE IS a puzzling and pervasive misconception in present-day thinking that the existence of God cannot be intellectually determined, and that mentally accepting the existence of God is strictly a matter of non-rational belief (faith).

As such, contemplating God's existence is erroneously regarded as the exclusive subject of faith-based or speculative ideologies (religion and philosophy) which have no proper place in natural scientific study.

The fact is, there are a number of very convincing intellectual arguments concerning the existence of God that have been around for hundreds of years. Indeed, the existence of God can be determined with compelling intellectual certainty—provided the thinker honestly wishes to do so. Moreover, recent advances and discoveries in science have not weakened previous intellectual arguments for God's existence, but instead have enormously strengthened and supported them.

Intellectually assenting to the existence of God is easily demonstrated to be a superlatively logical conclusion, not some vague irrational conceptualization. Remarkably, at the present time there are only two seriously competing intellectual explanations of life: the existence of God (the "God-hypothesis") and the existence of infinite universes (the "multiverse theory"). The postulation of an infinite number of unobservable universes is clearly a desperate attempt by atheistic scientists to avoid the God-hypothesis as the most credible and logical intellectual explanation of life and the universe. Moreover, under intellectual scrutiny, the scientifically celebrated "evolutionary theory" is here demonstrated to be fatally-flawed (philosophically illogical) as a credible explanation of life.

In this particular discourse, five well-known intellectual arguments for God's existence will be thoroughly examined. In considering these arguments, every attempt has been made to include current contributions, advances and discoveries that have modernized the more traditional arguments. Prior to examining these particular arguments for God, the universal predilection to establish intellectual 'oneness'—"monism"—will be considered in detail as well as the recurring propensity to postulate the existence of one supreme being—"monotheism."

Once intellectual certainty of one Supreme Being is established, a number of divine attributes can be logically deduced as well. Eleven of these attributes will be determined and examined in greater detail.

FOR COUNTLESS esoteric students today, the Mystery centres of ancient times have retained a powerful and fascinating allure. Moreover, there is often a wishful longing to revive and continue their secretive initiatory activity into modern times.

Unfortunately, this anachronistic longing is largely based on an illusionary misunderstanding of these Mysteries and the real reasons for their destined demise.

The primary reason for the disappearance of the ancient Mysteries is that they have been supplanted by the superior new mysteries—the mysteries of the Son. These new mysteries were initiated by Christ-Jesus himself. In order to better understand these Son-mysteries in a spiritually-scientific way, Rudolf Steiner (1861–1925) established the Anthroposophical Movement and Society.

Unfortunately, anthroposophy today has become unduly influenced by members and leaders who long to transform spiritual science into a modern-day Mystery institution. Moreover, contrary to his own words and intentions, Rudolf Steiner is even claimed to be the founder of some new "Michael-Mysteries."

By carefully establishing a correct esoteric understanding of the ancient pagan Mysteries, as well as a better appreciation of the new mysteries of the Son, this well-researched and readable discourse convincingly shows that all current and past attempts to revive the ancient pagan Mysteries regressively diverts human development backward to the seducer of mankind, Lucifer, rather than progressively forward to the saviour of mankind, Christ-Jesus.

Moreover, by additionally tracing the intriguing historical

development of esoteric Christianity (particularly the Knights of the Holy Grail and Rosicrucianism) alongside Freemasonry, the Knights Templar and Theosophy, this important and necessary study illuminates the correct esoteric position and true significance of anthroposophical spiritual science.

This book is available to order from Amazon.com

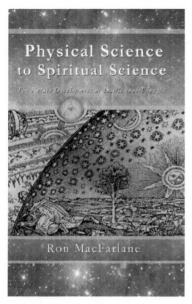

THE PRIDE OF civilized mankind—intellectual thinking—is at a critical crossroads today. No doubt surprising to many, the cognitive capacity to consciously formulate abstract ideas in the mind, and then to manipulate them according to devised rules of logic in order to acquire new knowledge has only been humanly possible for about the last 3,000 years. Prior to intellectual (abstract) thinking, mental activity characteristically consisted of vivid pictorial images that arose spontaneously in the human mind from natural and supernatural stimuli.

The ability to think abstractly is the necessary foundation for mathematics, language and empirical science. The developmental history of intellectual thought, then, exactly parallels the developmental history of mathematics, language and science. Moreover, since abstract thinking inherently encourages the cognitive separation of subject (the thinker) and object (the perceived environment), the history of intellectual development also parallels the historical development of self-conscious (ego) awareness.

Over the last 3000 years, mankind in general has slowly perfected intellectual thinking, and thereby developed complex mathematics, sophisticated languages, comprehensively-detailed empirical sciences and pronounced ego-awareness. Unfortunately, all this intellectual activity over the many previous centuries has also exclusively strengthened human awareness of the physical, material world and substantially decreased awareness of the superphysical, spiritual world.

That is why today, intellectual thinking is at a critical crossroads in further development. Thinking (intellectual or otherwise) is a superphysical activity—an activity within the soul. Empirical science is incorrect in postulating that physical brain tissue generates thought. The brain is simply the biological "sending and receiving" apparatus: sending sense-perceptions to the soul and receiving thought-conceptions from the soul. All this activity certainly generates chemical and electrical activity within the brain; but this activity is the effect, not the cause of thinking.

The danger to future intellectual thought is that increased acceptance of the erroneous scientific notion that thinking is simply brain-chemistry will increasingly deny and deaden true superphysical thinking. Future thinking runs the risk of becoming "a self-fulfilled prophecy"—the more people fervently believe that thought is simply brain-chemistry, the more thought will indeed become simply brain-chemistry. As a result, future human beings will be less responsible for generating their own thinking activity and more involuntarily controlled by their own brain chemistry. The artificial intelligence of machines won't become more human; but instead human beings will become more like robotic machines.

Presently, then, empirical science is leading intellectual thinking in a downward, materialistic direction. Correspondingly, however, true spiritual science (anthroposophy) is also actively engaged in leading intellectual thought back to its superphysical source in the soul. *Physical Science to Spiritual Science: the Future Development of Intellectual Thought* begins by examining the historical development of intellectual thinking and the corresponding rise of physical science. Once this has been discussed, practical and detailed information is presented on how spiritual science is leading intellectual thinking back to its true soul-source. It is intended that upon completion of this discourse, sincere and open-minded readers will themselves come to experience the exhilarating, superphysical nature of their own intellectual thought.

This book is available to order from Amazon.com

THE DIVINE TRINITY—the greatest of all Christian mysteries. How is it that the one God is a unity of three divine persons? Christ-Jesus first revealed this mystery to his disciples when on earth. Later, around the sixth century, the Trinitarian mystery was theologically clarified and outlined by the formulation of the Athanasian Creed. Conceptual understanding of the divine Trinity has changed very little in Western society since then. Similarly theological understanding of the Logos-Word, as mentioned in the Gospel of St. John. The traditional understanding, that has remained essentially unchallenged for centuries, is that the Logos-Word is synonymous with God the Son. As for creation, the best that mainstream Christianity has historically provided is an ancient, allegorical account contained in the Book of Genesis.

Out of the hidden well-springs of esoteric Christianity, and as the title indicates, *The Greater Mysteries of the Divine Trinity, the Logos-Word and Creation*, delves much more deeply into the profound mysteries of the Trinitarian God, the Logos-Word of St. John and the creation of the universe. The divine Trinity is here demonstrated to be the loving union of Heavenly Father, Holy Mother and Eternal Son. The Logos-Word is here evidenced to be the "Universal Man," the primordial, cosmic creation of God the Son. Universal creation itself is here detailed to be the "one life becoming many"—the multiplication of the Logos-Word into countless individualized life-forms and beings.

The depth and breadth of original and thought-provoking information presented here will, no doubt, stimulate and excite those esoteric thinkers who are seriously seeking answers to the deeper mysteries of life, existence and the universe.

This book is available to order from Amazon.com

Also check out the authour's website:

www.heartofshambhala.com

A Site Dedicated to True Esoteric Christianity

WHEN CHRIST-JESUS walked the earth over two thousand years ago, he established a two-fold division in his teaching that has continued to this day. To the general public, he simplified his teaching and presented it in pictorial, allegorical and figurative imagery in the form of stories, parables and lessons that could be imaginatively and intuitively understood.

To his inner circle of disciples (who were sufficiently prepared), however, he taught intellectual concepts, clear ideas and logical reasoning that could be understood on a much deeper and wider level of comprehension. As biblically explained:

> Then the disciples came and said to him, "Why do you speak to them [the general public] in parables?" And he answered them, "To you it has been given to know the secrets of the kingdom of heaven, but to them it has not been given ... This is why I speak to them in parables, because seeing they do not see, and hearing they do not hear, nor do they understand." (Matt 13:10, 13)

Moreover, in union with the divine, Our Saviour was able to reveal sacred knowledge that had never been previously presented in the entire history of mankind: "I will explain mysteries hidden since the creation of the world" (Matt 13:35). This sacred and revealed knowledge has been termed "Christ-mysteries" or "mysteries of the Son."

After his glorious resurrection and ascension, Christ-Jesus institutionalized his two-fold mystery-teachings through St. Peter and St. John (the evangelist, not the apostle). Through St. Peter, Our Saviour instituted a universal, Christian *religion* and *theology* to preserve, promote and convey the more basic and simplified mystery-teachings that are intended for the general public. Through St. John, Christ-Jesus instituted a universal, Christian *philosophy* and *theosophy* to preserve, promote and convey the more comprehensive and complex mystery-teachings that are intended for the more advanced disciples (Christian initiates). In esoteric terminology, the institutionalized teachings through St. Peter are known as the "lesser mysteries of exoteric Christianity." The institutionalized teachings through St. John are known as the "greater mysteries of esoteric Christianity."

While both mystery-teaching approaches are equally sacred, profound and intended to complement each other, corrupt and intolerant authorities within the universal institution (Church) of St. Peter, for many centuries, persecuted and attacked any public expressions of esoteric Christianity. Consequently, genuine historical forms of esoteric Christianity, such as the Knights of the Holy Grail and the Fraternity of the Rose-Cross, were forced to be secretive and publically-hidden during the past two thousand years.

Thankfully today, the social, political and intellectual climate has progressed to the point where the greater mystery-teachings of esoteric Christianity can begin to be publically revealed for the first time. This modern-day outpouring really began with the twentieth-century establishment of anthroposophy by Rudolf Steiner (1861–1925). The information and approach presented in *The Star of Knowledge: The Five Guiding Mysteries of Esoteric Christianity*, is intended to augment and continue the mystery-teachings of Christ-Jesus as safeguarded by the Rosicrucian Fraternity and publicized through anthroposophy.

Consequently, this particular discourse delves much more deeply and comprehensively into the cosmos-changing, salvational achievement of Christ-Jesus: the historical and cosmic preparations; as well as his birth, life, death, resurrection and ascension. While much of this mystery information may be unfamiliar, unknown and unexpected to mainstream (exoteric) Christianity, it in no way is meant to criticize, denigrate or displace the profound teachings of the universal Church; but rather, to complement, to enhance and to enlarge—for the betterment of true Christianity and, thereby, the betterment of all mankind.

This book is available to order from Amazon.com

Made in the USA
Lexington, KY
24 April 2017